Rethinking Russia's National Interests

SIGNIFICANT ISSUES SERIES papers are written for and published by the Center for Strategic and International Studies.

Series Editors: David M. Abshire
                 Douglas M. Johnston

Director of Studies: Erik R. Peterson

Director of Publications: Nancy B. Eddy

Managing Editor: Roberta L. Howard

Associate Editor: Yoma Ullman

The Center for Strategic and International Studies (CSIS), founded in 1962, is an independent, tax-exempt, public policy research institution based in Washington, D.C. The mission of the Center is to advance the understanding of emerging world issues in the areas of international economics, politics, security, and business. It does so by providing a strategic perspective to decision makers that is integrative in nature, international in scope, anticipatory in its timing, and bipartisan in its approach. The Center's commitment is to serve the common interests and values of the United States and other countries around the world that support representative government and the rule of law.

CSIS, as an independent research institution, does not take specific public policy positions. All views, positions, and conclusions expressed in this publication should be understood to be solely those of the individual authors and not necessarily those of their parent institutions.

Center for Strategic and International Studies
1800 K Street, N.W., Suite 400
Washington, D.C. 20006
Telephone: (202) 887-0200
Fax: (202) 775-3199

Rethinking Russia's National Interests

edited by Stephen Sestanovich

Center for Strategic
and International Studies
Washington, D.C.

Library of Congress Cataloging-in-Publication Data

Rethinking Russia's national interests / edited and with a foreword by
    Stephen Sestanovich
        p. cm. — (Significant issues series, ISSN 0736-7136 ; v. 16, no. 1)
        Includes bibliographical references.
        ISBN 0-89206-221-5
        1. Russia (Federation)—Foreign relations.   2. Nationalism—Russia
(Federation).   3. United States—Foreign relations—Russia (Federation).
4. Russia (Federation)—Foreign relations—United States.   I. Sestanovich,
Stephen, 1950-.   II. Center for Strategic and International Studies (Washington, D.C.)   III. Series.
DK510.764.R48   1994
327.47—dc20   93-40403
                                                                          CIP

Significant Issues Series, Volume XVI, Number 1
© 1994 by the Center for Strategic and International Studies
Washington, D.C. 20006
All rights reserved
Printed on recycled paper in the United States of America

Contents

About the Contributors

Anders Åslund is professor and director of the Stockholm Institute of East European Economics at the Stockholm School of Economics and author of *Post-Communist Economic Revolutions* and *Gorbachev's Struggle for Economic Reform.*

Francis Fukuyama is a resident consultant at the RAND Corporation in Washington, D.C., and author of *The End of History and the Last Man.*

Paul A. Goble is a senior fellow at the Carnegie Endowment for International Peace in Washington, D.C.

Henry A. Kissinger is a counselor at the Center for Strategic and International Studies in Washington, D.C., and former secretary of state.

Vladimir P. Lukin is ambassador to the United States for the Russian Federation.

Sergei Rogov is head of the Center for National Security and International Relations and deputy director of the Institute for the Study of the USA and Canada, Russian Federation Academy of Sciences.

Stephen Sestanovich is director of Russian and Eurasian Studies at the Center for Strategic and International Studies in Washington, D.C.

Aleksandr Shokhin is a deputy prime minister of the Russian Federation.

Sergei B. Stankevich is a former presidential adviser to Boris Yeltsin.

Nikolai Travkin is founder of the Democratic Party of Russia.

Paul D. Wolfowitz is dean of the Paul H. Nitze School of Advanced International Studies at the Johns Hopkins University and former under secretary of defense.

Foreword

Among the many twists and turns of post-Communist political terminology, few are more revealing than the changing uses of the expression *national interest.* In the late 1980s, when Mikhail Gorbachev and Eduard Shevardnadze introduced the term into official discussions of Soviet foreign policy, they clearly regarded it as a lever with which to free diplomacy from the weight of Marxist-Leninist ideology. The Western term was a symbol of a much broader "Westernization" of Soviet policy. Immediately after the Soviet Union's collapse, by contrast, the defense of "national interest" became the slogan of conservative Russian nationalists, who insisted that their country's distinctive needs and purposes were being sacrificed to the tyranny of inappropriate internationalist ideas — this time, those of liberal democracy and capitalism. Those who make this argument doubtless feel that the December 1993 parliamentary elections gave them a boost, but the struggle over how to define Russia's interests is far from over. Foreign Minister Andrei Kozyrev has responded to critics by saying that what conservatives "offer under the guise of patriotism is the sellout of our national interests."

Even in the West, the "national interest" has always been, at best, a work in progress — a subject of seemingly permanent disagreement. At any one moment, there are those who consider that the "national interest" requires a more ambitious foreign policy; others, that it dictates a less ambitious one. But Russia's debate on this issue is especially hard to resolve, for (as many of the essays in this volume suggest) it has to begin with the most basic question: What nation are we talking about? The Soviet Union of old, or the new Russia? Many nations can find different definitions of themselves by consulting their history, but it is a very rare case in which the principal alternative to the status quo is so recent (the Soviet Union, after all, is only two years in the past), so different from current reality (it was nearly twice as populous as today's Russian Federation of 150 million people), and so charged in its international implications (talk of reconstituting the USSR challenges the independence of no less than 14 sovereign states).

Agreement on Russia's national interests, then, awaits agreement on its national identity. This is abundantly clear in debate about what all Russians agree is the central question they have to resolve — the nature of their relations with the "near abroad," those states formed out of the old Soviet Union.

The debate starts with a disagreement about ends. For some, the appropriate goals of Russian policy for the "near abroad" are quite concrete and practical. Russia's interest in the status of Russian minorities in neighboring states, for example, requires constant attention to the citizenship laws under which these people live, to employment practices, to educational opportunities, and so on. These are problems, in other words, that call for problem-solving. But for other participants in Russia's debate, no such solutions can be sufficient. The mere fact that relations between Russia and its new neighbors are those of separate states, even if linked in a commonwealth, is simply too difficult to accept. The result is a search for various kinds of "special relationships," ranging from confederation to full union.

Just as the proper ends of Russian policy are disputed, so is the proper relationship between ends and means. Russians have grown accustomed to the notion that they have to scale back their goals because their power as a nation is less formidable than it seemed, at least, in the Soviet past. It was Gorbachev himself who gently scolded the 1986 Communist Party Congress with the warning that the Soviet Union had to temper what he called the "grandeur" of its aims with realism about its capabilities. Because these capabilities were in decline, many who could not on ideological grounds accept the retreat from Afghanistan, or the loss of empire in Eastern Europe, resigned themselves to the inevitable.

The same awareness of political, financial, and other constraints is a continuing source of moderation in Russian foreign policy. It produces practical agreement among those whose principles still clash. It should be added, however, that these constraints seem far less acute when it comes to the "near abroad" than they do in Russia's policy toward other parts of the world. The internal disarray of most of Russia's new neighbors — their just-created political institutions, their disintegrating economies, their often-fictitious military establishments — means that enhancing Russian influence over them looks more affordable than many of the foreign policy projects of the old regime did. The vast Soviet empire proved an unbearable burden; the costs of a "sphere of influence" may be much less great.

There is no doubt that Russians feel a renewed confidence in their ability to manage their relations with the "near abroad." At the same time, recent events confirm that there is no agreement about what costs are bearable even in dealing with former Soviet states. The widespread objections within the Yeltsin government in the fall of 1993 to the creation of a "ruble zone" — on grounds that it would disrupt domestic economic reform — were proof that cost remains a serious obstacle to the revival of imperial thinking.

When we speak of foreign policy debates, and of controversies over such matters as interests and identity or ends and means, it is easy to forget that we are not talking about a national seminar. The "answers" that Russia is searching for will be judged — both at home and abroad — less by their intellectual coherence than by their political sustainability. In fact, policies that strike a workable balance may emerge even if a clear set of principles does not. The fact that Russian foreign policy debate became slightly less rancorous in 1993 than in 1992 is perhaps a sign that this balance is already being struck.

Yet even if there is some movement toward a provisional consensus, there can be little certainty about what policies will sustain a consensus in the future. The civil war in Tajikistan, for example, has produced very little real disagreement among Russians. Intervention in Uzbekistan and Kazakhstan would be different (both from the Tajik case and from each other), and Ukraine would be another matter altogether.

Each of these cases will be judged differently, not only because each country presents very different problems and opportunities for Russia but because Russia itself is changing. As the 1993 parliamentary elections showed, the rapid pace of political developments brings new participants, new institutions, new slogans to the fore. Each round of debate about national interests is, in effect, conducted by a different country.

The essays in this volume represent an attempt — or rather, many attempts — to understand and contribute to Russia's unfolding debate about its interests in the international arena. For the reader, they offer an opportunity to encounter the views of an exceptionally diverse group of Russian policymakers, politicians, and intellectuals. All five Russian contributors presented themselves as candidates for parliament in December 1993. Vladimir Lukin, Russia's ambassador to the United States since early 1992, was a leader of one of the most important groups contesting those elections, the so-called Yavlinsky-Boldyrev-Lukin bloc. Sergei Stankevich and Aleksandr Shokhin, who served President Boris Yeltsin as counselor and as deputy prime minister, respectively, became two of the top figures of the Party of Russian Unity and Accord. Nikolai Travkin is the leader of the Democratic Party of Russia, and Sergei Rogov is a principal adviser on foreign policy to the Civic Union, led by Arkady Volsky.

It should be added that the Western contributors to this volume, while they cannot quite be called "participants" in the Russian debate, are among the most influential outsiders whose views (whether they are considered friendly or hostile) are taken into account by Russians themselves.

All the essays in this collection were first presented at a conference entitled "Russia's National Interests: An International Dialogue," held in Moscow in October 1992 under the joint sponsorship of the Center for Strategic and International Studies and the Moscow-based Center for National Security and International Relations. The staff of the latter center, and its director, Sergei Rogov, provided indispensable help in solving one problem after another.

Similar thanks are due to Henry Kissinger and Vladimir Lukin, who as cochairmen of the conference kept the proceedings lively, rigorous, and at times even orderly; and to David Kramer and Alexander Guroff of CSIS, who helped with the editing and revision of the papers.

Finally, we acknowledge our special debt to the John M. Olin Foundation, Inc., The Starr Foundation, and the Prince Charitable Trusts, whose generous help made the project possible.

Stephen Sestanovich
Director of Russian and Eurasian Studies
CSIS, Washington, D.C.
December 1993

1

Russian and American Interests after the Cold War

Henry A. Kissinger

The end of the cold war presents all major states with a world totally different from any they have experienced. Russia lives within borders that it has not had since before Peter the Great. The United States is in the position that George Bernard Shaw once described: "There are two tragedies in life—one is to lose your heart's desire. The other is to gain it." America has achieved everything it set out to do 50 years ago. The result, however, is that it now finds itself in a world for which it has no historical or perhaps even intellectual preparation. In essence, we are flying blind.

As for Europe, it had become used to the division of Germany, which created a certain equilibrium in which the growing strength of the Federal Republic was, to some extent, subordinated to the need to gain legitimacy: Germany's strength was balanced by Germany's need for political acceptance. Now Germany no longer has any need to make concessions not justified by its perception of the balance of forces. And Europe, no longer fearing the Soviet Union, no longer feels the same imperative to move in the direction of the technocratic approach to European unity in which bureaucrats in Brussels prescribe certain formulas.

All of this means there is in central Europe a recurrence of nationalism and other tendencies that have not been seen in many years. Some of these trends, oddly enough, resemble the period of 1900 to 1914. Others resemble the period of 1930 to 1940. This is not to express doubts about the present German government or about Chancellor Helmut Kohl, in whom I have enormous confidence. But there is a structural comparison that is worth thinking about.

As for the developing nations, the end of the cold war affects them too. They had built a policy of nonalignment on the existence of two camps. But what does nonalignment mean in a world in which there are no longer two superpowers? At the nonaligned conference in Jakarta in September 1992, participants had a diffi-

1

cult time trying to define a program for 107 nations that could no longer play off two blocs against each other.

A global transformation is under way, and nowhere are the changes more important than in relations between Russia and the United States. What is the right way to look at this relationship? My own view of international affairs is sometimes attacked in the United States as being unprincipled, amoral, uninterested in values, and so forth. This is not the place to resume that particular debate, except to say that the final test of a foreign policy is whether it shows an understanding of the trends of history. Bismarck once said that the best a statesman can do is to listen carefully to the footsteps of God, try to get hold of a corner of his cloak, and follow a few steps of the way in that direction. For statesmen there is no one slogan that encompasses all of reality. They face issues that do not present themselves in black and white categories.

Nations are formed by their history, by their geography, by cultural legacies. If a nation has done something for 400 years, it indicates a certain proclivity; it means that for 400 years its actions have appeared reasonable to successive generations of the leading people of that society.

Because such legacies matter, we should recognize that the American and Russian experiences have been totally different. The United States is the only nation ever to be created in constant pursuit of the idea of liberty. It is the only country to which people could come to create a system that avowedly had no precedent. It is the only nation that until very recently has never had a security problem. It is a nation that had a powerful internal consensus and no physical threat from the outside world. No other nation in history has ever had that experience. It was therefore absolutely natural for the United States to develop the conception that what it did was its own justification. Americans saw their country as a beacon of liberty that could change events all over the world; it did not have to do anything but live by its own values.

There have always been two versions of American isolationism. One saw the United States as too good for the world: it therefore should not defile itself by contact with others. The second version held that America had to prove itself before it had a moral right to participate in the world's affairs. We have seen both of these versions in action in our own lifetime. That is the American experience.

The Russian experience has been very different. Here is a country that has never had a friendly neighbor, that has always had shifting borders, that has never had a clearly defined security arrangement—a country, quite frankly, that has been either too weak or too strong for the peace of Europe, a country that at one and the same time has been a central element of the balance of power and a threat to it.

Like the United States, Russia has had a great belief in its spiritual mission. What emerges from the pages of the great novelists like Dostoyevsky is a belief that the peculiar suffering of the Russian people has produced a spirituality compared to which Europe is materialistic and small-minded. (The United States has been so far away that it really plays no role in this philosophical perception.) Where the American approach was missionary, the Russian approach was exclusive: if you had not suffered, if you had not gone through the Russian experience, you could not really understand the Russian outlook.

These two countries have never found it all that easy to understand each other. Russian history has led to a very understandable concern for security because Russia has lived in a geography that set no natural boundaries. In the late nineteenth century, a Russian statesman once said, "We have now reached Odessa, but if we do not reach the Adriatic, we will have to return to the Dnieper." This is not aggressiveness in the normal sense; it is a sense of boundlessness. And Russia has exhibited a curious phenomenon: almost every offensive war that it has fought has ended badly, and every defensive war victoriously—a paradox.

The difference in the thinking of Americans and Russians has shown itself again and again. In May 1942, Stalin sent Vyacheslav Molotov to the United States to discuss the end of the war. At that time, the United States had the strongest bargaining position it was ever going to have; it was the time to set conditions. But Franklin Roosevelt thought that to insist on conditions in wartime would destroy Allied harmony; he did not want to bargain. The same pattern was repeated in Tehran in 1943. It was almost a philosophical matter: for Americans, harmony and cooperation were ends in themselves.

To most other societies, successful foreign policy is measured by concrete achievement. Americans believe in foreign policy by conversion. They tend to think that if there is discord, it must be due to evil—an evil person or an evil system, which has to be destroyed. But they also believe that evil can be overcome: if you take Nikita Khrushchev to a grain field in Iowa, if you call Stalin "Uncle Joe," if you show another Russian leader that we have swimming pools, you will discover in the end that the Russians are really midwestern Americans. Such thinking is not unlike that of a friend of mine who is of the view that there is no such thing as an English accent: the accent, he believes, is simply put on to intimidate Americans, and therefore if you can catch an Englishman unawares, say, by calling him at four in the morning, he will talk like a normal human being.

Americans are greatly tempted by what one can call American triumphalism. Some say to themselves, "We have prevailed because of the purity of our ideas, and if we only improve ourselves strenuously the whole world will be persuaded by the excellence of our maxims. We need no foreign policy other than the strenuous practice of democratic values, and everything else will fall in place."

This view obviously produces a kind of paternalism in relations with others. It leads to overextension and domestic frustration. It makes clear how much the United States needs an agreed concept of its national interest. That is, America has to be able to explain—to itself and others—why it does certain things, for what reason, and at what cost.

Reading the inaugural addresses of American presidents in this century shows that, if they talk about foreign policy at all, they always say something like this: "We Americans have no selfish interests in the world. We act only on behalf of others. We stand for universal principles, for the rule of law, for collective security, but God forbid that we should want anything for ourselves." There are variations on this message, but at bottom it is always the same.

American presidents do not understand that this makes other nations extremely nervous, because such an altruistic foreign policy is extremely changeable. It is much easier to calculate what a nation wants to do for its own purposes—what its national interest is. It does not much matter *how* that interest is defined. But it needs to be precise, concrete, and calculable so that Americans and other people in the world can work with it.

This is the American challenge at present, and it is especially acute because so much has changed. No one in the United States thought that Communism would collapse so rapidly. It used to be said it would collapse eventually, but that was a kind of liturgy. The idea that the Russian empire created since the reign of Peter the Great would disintegrate has not been a part of even the most far-out reflections on the possible evolution of international affairs. The U.S. government once hesitated even to talk about the independence of the Baltic states, whose conquest it had never recognized. Now it has to deal with Ukraine and Uzbekistan, places familiar not even to one half of one percent of Americans.

Let me turn to the Russian challenge. The collapse of the old order presents several huge challenges to the former Soviet Union. The first of these—the collapse of Communism—is largely an economic problem because, in my sacrilegious view, Communism collapsed above all because of its total failure to create a workable modern economy. In a system in which everything moved by allocation, the only real market was the selling of favors; corruption was inevitable, and what emerged was a new feudal class.

The problem now is how to move from a centrally planned system, which creates a certain set of expectations, to a market economy. In a centrally planned system managers are not entrepreneurs but bureaucrats; they operate in a system every part of which has an arrangement with every other part, so that the top echelon has the greatest difficulty finding out what is going on. How do you create a market system when you have to use most of the same people who ran the old system and when there is no obvious alternative? That is a huge problem to which we in the West can contribute a little money, some advice, a lot of compassion, and a little self-restraint.

In post-Communist Russia, the economy is the first but not the hardest challenge. The biggest problem Russia faces—and the biggest one the United States will face in dealing with Russia, even though it does not fully understand it yet—concerns Russia's relations with the other former Soviet states. For Russia, those lands that had always been considered part of Russia, indeed from which Russia originated, like Ukraine, are now foreign countries, and they deal with Moscow as a security problem. That is a huge emotional adjustment.

Sergei Rogov's essay in this book illustrates this issue. When he describes how the Russian army is being established, he refers to the fact that conscription notices are sent out all over the former Soviet Union. Russian conscripts, he notes, are assured that they do not have to serve in Central Asia. But the conscripts in other parts of the former Soviet Union may well have to serve there; they are not given any such assurance. Consider: Where else could it happen that a sovereign nation conscripts people from other sovereign nations to serve in yet third sovereign nations and nobody considers this a little odd?

This is not the only peculiar development. When the American press reports what the Russian 14th Army is doing in Moldova, the only reason that no eyebrows are raised is that most Americans do not know where Moldova is. They certainly do not know that Ukraine lies between Moldova and Russia. Nobody asks, "What is the Russian 14th Army doing in Moldova?" I am not criticizing its role there, but it does represent a potential problem.

Future good relations between Russia and the United States depend to an important degree on mutual recognition—in particular Russian recognition—that Russia's borders are recognized international borders and that Russia's relations with other erstwhile components of the former Soviet Union will be relations with foreign countries. This is not to say that the United States is against close and cooperative relations among those states. It will hardly question that Russia has special concerns in the areas close to it, just as the United States has special concerns in the Western Hemisphere. The United States has created a free trade agreement with Mexico; it is for the former Soviet states to make similar agreements among themselves. It may also be possible to create among the members of the post-Soviet Commonwealth something like the relationships between members of the European Community as well as alliances and other collective security arrangements. In that event, Western concerns about Russia's objectives will be greatly eased.

The alternatives are very clear in the case of Central Asia. The interests of the United States in Central Asia are largely parallel to the interests of Russia. The United States has absolutely no interest in seeing the spread of fundamentalism in the Central Asian republics. Quite the contrary, it has a strong interest in preventing it, as does Russia. The outside powers with an interest in this region—Turkey, Iran, Russia, the United States, maybe the People's Republic of China to some degree—will be on the same side most of the time. In fact, I cannot imagine when that would *not* be the case. Yet if the Russian army were to reoccupy the Central Asian countries in pursuit of traditional imperialist objectives, there would sooner or later be a massive collision between Russia and the United States. Even those like me who say "Keep in mind that Russia is a permanent great nation, not a missionary object" would oppose such actions.

Today, there are those who question whether the frontiers left to Russia by the collapse of the Soviet Union are in fact legitimate international borders. It is said, "These borders are simply the legacy of Lenin, Trotsky, and Stalin. Why should they be considered genuine Russian frontiers?" My answer is this: These are internationally established borders, recognized by the United Nations, and whatever historical analysis may show about how they came to be drawn where they are, changing them by force creates an international problem.

Many intellectual commentators like to say that peaceful changes of frontiers are all right. Unfortunately, I do not know of any examples of significant changes of frontiers by peaceful means. If it can be done, the United States certainly has no objection to it. But if these frontiers are changed by force, and if a Yugoslav-type situation develops on the territory of the former Soviet Union, there should be no illusions about the American response. The U.S. Congress and American public opinion will create a renewed state of extreme tension between Russia and the United States.

In the broadest sense, the United States wants Russia to see that a great state can live in security and prosperity in a world in which big buffer areas do not have the strategic value they once did. As Francis Fukuyama points out in his essay, the meaning of the national interest is no longer what it used to be: after all, a country like Japan, with next to no resources, has developed into an economic superpower on its own territory.

I am asked constantly whether the United States wants Russia weak. It is not a serious question. It is not in America's power to keep Russia weak. No other nation has gone through so much adversity and come back from so many tribulations, almost always by its own efforts. After the war of 1905, the situation of Russia was desperate. And yet by 1914 both the German and the Japanese general staffs had independently concluded that Russia was becoming so strong that in another five years it would defeat them unaided. That was not necessarily the right judgment, as World War I showed, but it suggested how quickly Russia had come back. Recovery will not be all that quick this time. It will be extremely difficult, but it is not an American option to keep Russia weak and cannot be seriously discussed.

In their new relationship, Russians and Americans can talk about many things: economic development, banking reform, private structures. These are all worthy subjects, but sooner or later they will have to talk to each other like two great nations. Indeed, the United States should talk to Russia about those subjects that will shape their joint future, and relations among the former Soviet states are one of the most important. As Paul Wolfowitz argues in this book, the United States is also asking basic questions about its policies in both Asia and Europe. It is clearly heading into a multipolar world, which presents it with new and unfamiliar difficulties. Americans have in the past been able to orient themselves on the basis of absolute good confronting absolute evil. If that outlook was not exactly accurate, it was close enough and did no great harm. Now, for the first time they have to orient themselves on the basis of relative dangers. As America considers its policy toward Germany, or the PRC, or the other major international actors, it should become clear that in all these cases Russian interests do not conflict in any significant way with those of the United States. This convergence can be the basis for a very serious discussion about how each side intends to go about defending those interests.

Such a discussion will help Americans to understand better the concerns that are such a prominent part of contemporary Russian debate. The treatment of minorities is the outstanding case. If this is primarily a humanitarian problem, the United States will find Russian policy easy enough to deal with. But if the concern for Russians living beyond Russia's current borders is a pretext for long-term recentralization, then it will demand a very different U.S. response.

The debate about these matters cannot be avoided. Both sides are going to find the new world difficult, in different ways. Russia has monumental problems, arising from the fact that more than 70 years of Communist rule and 400 years of expansion are being shredded. Given the scale of these problems, in fact, some people assume that Russia is doomed to repeat its history. I disagree. But the Russian people have huge choices to make that Americans cannot make for them. What America can do is begin treating Russia like a great nation.

The immediate problems of the United States are far less weighty, but it too has to adjust its thinking. Americans will have to make the same effort that the Russians are making to arrive at a realistic and sustainable conception of their national interest.

Meetings between the presidents of Russia and the United States are an opportunity to talk about what is most worrying to each side as it looks out over the next several years. President Clinton and President Yeltsin obviously have to address a longer and more complete list of issues than I have presented here. But even before they take up specific issues, they need to make a great step forward: they must be ready to deal with the issues that will decide their future over the long term and to do so on the basis of mutual respect.

2
The Ambiguity of "National Interest"

Francis Fukuyama

In the wake of the collapse of Communism and the breakup of the Soviet Union, it is only natural that there should be considerable interest in the question of Russian "national interests." Indeed, the new Russian state has been forced into such a debate because Marxist-Leninist ideology no longer serves to define its overall goals, while the very borders and geopolitical position of the country have changed dramatically. It is not often that states have this kind of opportunity—many would say misfortune—to remake themselves and their self-conceptions so thoroughly, unencumbered by preexisting domestic institutional structures or external commitments. For precedents, one has to look at what happened to other imperial centers like Turkey or Austria when their empires collapsed.

In the context of such a debate, it is a common temptation to argue that such a thing as a core or "objective" national interest exists that can serve as a guide or objective for foreign policy. Ideology can frequently induce states to seek unusual or extraordinary goals, like "building socialism" or "defending freedom" in some distant, strategically insignificant country in Africa or Asia. It would seem natural that as a country "de-ideologized" and became once again an "ordinary" nation, it would seek to strip itself of such universalistic goals in favor of the particularlistic ones that are, nonetheless, universally necessary for states.

An example of such thinking is Ambassador Vladimir Lukin's 1992 article in *Foreign Policy* in which he describes three schools of thought in the current Russian debate. The first he calls "ideologized democratic internationalism," in which Russian national interests are deliberately suppressed in favor of universalistic ones (this time, though, of a democratic rather than a socialist flavor); the second is a crude, revanchist Russian chauvinism; and the third (which he obviously prefers) is Russian national interest "properly understood."[1]

10

What is usually meant by a "proper" understanding of national interest is akin to the way the great powers of the nineteenth century understood it—that is, the maximization of a nation's power and influence to preserve its own autonomy, delinked from any overtly ideological foreign policy goals.[2] At times, this concept of national interest shades into what might be called "nationalist interest"—that is, the interest of the state's dominant national or ethnic group.

The belief that there is something like an objective national interest is by no means unique to Russians, however. Take an example much closer to home (my home, that is), the neo-conservative foreign policy journal *The National Interest,* founded by Irving Kristol and its present editor in chief, Owen Harries. An original motive for founding this magazine was the belief that U.S. foreign policy had been too long dominated by liberal internationalist goals like support for the United Nations (UN) and that America's extensive alliance commitments had outlived their usefulness. The founders hoped to stake out a conservative foreign policy agenda based on a much narrower and more *self*-interested concept of the U.S. national interest—in other words, the foreign policy of the United States as an "ordinary" country rather than the standard-bearer of the "free world."

In the end, however, I believe that all such attempts to define an objective national interest fail. True "core" national interests certainly exist but usually take a minimal role and are not terribly useful in defining a nation's foreign policy. Countries have a high degree of freedom in defining their national interest, and what passes for that interest in most contemporary discussions of the subject masks a host of ideological, political, historical, and cultural assumptions about national goals, the international environment, and the like. To say, therefore, that Russia or any other country should pursue its national interest still begs the question of what that national interest is. Worse, it introduces a covert nationalist agenda that may bring Russia into early conflict with its neighbors and with the rest of the international system. I will discuss the general problem of defining national interest in the contemporary world in the first section of this essay, and the specific problems of Russian national interest in the second.

The Changing Concept of National Interest

The idea that each nation could have something like a stable, objective national interest originated in the geopolitical theories of the nineteenth century and the European state system that spawned them. The traditional practice of realpolitik presumed that all states, regardless of regime, internal structure, religion, or the like, sought to defend their autonomy by maximizing their power vis-à-vis other states. The means by which a given state could do this, and the particular constraints under which it had to operate, were not subject to choice by its rulers, however, but were set by "objective" factors such as resources, population, and, above all, geography—that is, the state's position within the international state system. These unchanging environmental characteristics led to permanent interests and certain clear-cut rules for playing the balance-of-power game—for example, Britain's long-held dicta that it would oppose the rise of a hegemonic power on the Continent and defend the neutrality of the Low Countries. Indeed, the unchanging environment was held responsible for the internal character of states rather than the reverse: Prussia, it was argued, became a militarized garrison-state because of the constant pressure from enemies on all of its ill-defined and poorly defensible borders.

This kind of determinism-by-geography was codified in the latter part of the nineteenth century by geopolitical theorists like Mahan and McKinder. The more sophisticated view that a country's national interest is determined not by changeable internal factors but by the character of the international state system has been advanced in more recent times by the so-called realists—such figures as Hans Morgenthau, George Kennan, and, of course, Henry Kissinger. Contemporary realists do not emphasize narrow questions of geography to nearly the extent of Mahan and McKinder but refer to broader issues like the bipolar or multipolar character of power and take into account the impact of technological change like the development of nuclear weapons.

Nations do in fact have a certain unchanging core of permanent interests imposed on them by geography and the external environment. The foreign policy of a country like Poland, bounded as it is on two sides by powerful and ambitious neighbors, cannot help but differ from that of a Japan or an England surrounded by water. Countries need military establishments to defend their borders; and when they cannot achieve defensible borders, they need powerful allies, or at least good relations with powerful neighbors; and they need access to and communications with the outside world. These imperatives apply whether countries are ruled by military dictators, liberal democrats, or communists.

But in the contemporary world this core of national interests is actually rather small and does not help to define much of a foreign policy agenda. What pass for national interest in most discussions of the subject are in fact broader goals defined by social tradition, ideology, or culture that are not, strictly speaking, vital to a country's national security.

Three countries that have dramatically redefined their national interests in this century—Turkey, Japan, and the United States itself—illustrate this point. The case of Turkey demonstrates that long-held imperialist traditions can be abandoned virtually overnight and replaced by a completely new and, in a sense, artificial set of nationalist traditions. It was, of course, Kemal Atatürk who oversaw the transition from the crumbling Ottoman Empire to the modern Turkish nation-state. This involved, in the first instance, the abolition of the caliphate, the proclamation of a Turkish republic, and the renunciation of Turkey's former universalistic pretensions to be the guardian and promoter of Islam. In this respect, there are obvious parallels between Turkey in the decade after World War I and the present situation of Russia.

But the narrower national interest that replaced the former universalism of the Ottoman Empire was by no means a given, and the final form that it took was shaped decisively by Atatürk himself. Enver Pasha and many other Young Turk leaders in fact promoted an alternative, "modern," post-Ottoman concept of Turkish national identity. This would have made Turkey the protector and promoter of the interests of ethnic Turks throughout the region, including those well beyond the boundaries of the former Ottoman Empire. It was only the force of Atatürk's personality that undercut these dreams of a new pan-Turkic or pan-Turanian empire and created for the country the concept of a "small Turkey"—that is, a compact nation-state geographically limited to Anatolia. Turkey under Atatürk's firm guidance gave up its interest in the millions of its coethnics living in Iran, the Transcaucasus, and what would become Soviet Central Asia in favor of the development of a modern nation-state at home.

Part of Atatürk's project included the redefinition of national identity in cultural rather than political terms, and to this end he spent considerable time toward the end of his career on "linguistic" research aimed at recovering a more genuine, pre-Islamic Turkish language. Atatürk was hardly a competent linguist, and much of the new Turkish identity that he supposedly "recovered" was in fact a complete fabrication. Still, it served the political objective of creating a Turkish national identity separate from those prevalent under the Ottomans or the Young Turks, those that linked Turkishness to either religion or empire.

Atatürk's feat was quite remarkable. Turkey withdrew as one of the European great powers and with remarkably little internal turmoil reconciled itself to a very modern concept of nationalism. One could say that this situation was simply imposed on Turkey by the collapse of its empire, but surely the transition to "ordinary" statehood would have been much more traumatic, costly, and bloody had someone like Enver Pasha, with his pan-Turkic dreams, emerged as the father of modern Turkey.

One can argue that the redefinition of national interest that took place in Turkey was eased by a number of factors that do not exist in Russia today. A genuine military hero, Atatürk had a degree of prestige in Turkey unparalleled by any present-day Russian leader. Moreover, proclamation of a small Turkey was preceded by a bloody war with Greece that in effect constituted an "ethnic cleansing" of the intermingled Greek and Turkish populations on either side of the Bosphorus, thereby making Anatolia itself considerably more homogeneous ethnically. One might further argue that Turkey is today no longer content with the goals set for it by Atatürk and that it is reviving earlier pan-Turkic ambitions in its forays into Central Asia. I do not believe the Atatürk legacy has in fact been abandoned; in any case, the point remains that the nature of the pared-down national interest that emerges after the renunciation of more universalistic goals is variable and by no means dictated by geography or convention.

The second case of radically changing national interest is Japan. Before World War II, Japan behaved in many ways like a typical European nineteenth-century great power, accumulating military power and building a territorial empire in Asia. After its defeat in 1945, Japan's considerable national energies were redirected from acquiring the traditional desiderata of great-power status toward internal economic growth. In the process, the postwar Japanese seem to have inadvertently invented a new kind of state power, a techno-nationalism based on the ownership of high value-added technologies rather than conventional real estate.

Japan became in many ways a highly abnormal state. It in effect turned over its national security to a foreign country (a country, moreover, that had recently defeated it in war), formally renounced the use of force (even in self-defense) in its constitution, and voluntarily accepted a wide range of restrictions on, among other actions, its right to arm itself and to produce and export weapons. Any of these conditions would normally be seen as a gross violation of national sovereignty, and yet to this day attempts by the leadership of the ruling coalition to return Japan to the status of a "normal" country capable of such modest undertakings as contributing peacekeeping forces to UN operations is strongly resisted by public opinion.

With Japan's emergence as a global economic superpower, there is growing pressure inside the country to change its status in the international community. Arguably, Japan is still striving to maximize its power—but through rapid economic growth rather than the accumulation of weapons. There is, however, a big difference between the imperialism of the gun and the imperialism of the yen. Although Japan, like Turkey, may one day seek to revive its openly imperialist past, the fact that it has successfully sought dramatically different kinds of national interests for the past 47 years has highly benefited the international system.

The final case of shifting national interests is the United States itself. The United States has moved between extremes of isolation and international involvement in this century, owing in part to changes in the external environment (for example, the attack on Pearl Harbor in 1941) but also in great measure to simple changes in attitudes concerning significant national interests. For example, since the establishment of the internationalist consensus in the early days of the cold war, most American elites took it for granted that the preservation of U.S. allies in Europe, Asia, and the Middle East constituted a vital U.S. interest. This led to costly and, at times, dangerous policies to defend them, and yet the real threat to U.S. security was almost never a direct one. In earlier periods, the United States had opted for a greater degree of isolationism and lived quite happily in such a world. The defense of allies reflected a vision of the sort of world the United States wanted to live in (i.e., a world open to U.S. economic interests and sharing democratic values) rather than any absolute security requirement. The United States is currently embarking on a debate over its own post-cold war foreign policy. In the 1992 election campaign, the poles of this debate stretched from the neo-isolationism of Pat Buchanan to the global neo-Wilsonianism of Bill Clinton.

The Uncertainty of Permanent National Interests

The reasons why permanent national interest can no longer be regarded as a reliable guide for foreign policy are related to the broader social changes that have occurred over the past 100 or so years. The first has to do with changing technology, particularly military technology. Technological advance has changed the importance of geography and resources, making some formerly worthless assets valuable while devaluing others. The so-called Northern Territories, for example, were of symbolic but little military value until the development of the nuclear-fueled ballistic missile submarine (SSBN) made access to patrol areas in the Sea of Okhotsk strategically significant. Sea power, which seemed so central in Mahan's view, has been devalued with the development of airplanes, ballistic missiles, and nuclear weapons. Geostrategic position, in other words, can be of uncertain or ambiguous meaning and subject to rapid erosion as a result of technological advance.

The second and more important factor undermining the concept of permanent national interest has to do with changing concepts of legitimacy. The classic goals of national interest for the great powers—the accumulation of power and the exercise of influence—actually grew out of the aristocratic social order of the traditional European state system. The shift from monarchical to nationalist and democratic concepts of legitimacy has dramatically altered the kinds of goals states set for themselves and the means by which they can achieve them. The simple shift from one form of legitimacy to another changes the state system and thereby the external environment that countries have to face—such was the situation after the Versailles settlement when the Hapsburg and Ottoman empires were replaced by a state system based on nationality—and it explains what is going on now in the former Soviet Union.

Nationalist concepts of legitimacy make it not only difficult but undesirable to hold on to territory inhabited by another ethnic group; on the other hand, they raise new objectives for uniting coethnics living under different political jurisdictions. Liberal democratic legitimacy tends to lead to an *embourgeoisement* of social life and of foreign policy, shifting goals away from military contests over prestige to economic objectives. Stable democracies sharing common concepts of democratic legitimacy have had a remarkable track record in not fighting one another,[3] and although they may compete in the economic arena (witness the bad feelings in Europe over the currency crisis in late 1992), they are not preoccupied in the classical sense with maximizing power in their relations with each other.

The final reason why it is hard to define permanent national interests has to do with changes in the nature of economic production. Up through the early phases of the industrial revolution, a country's power was largely determined by its territory, resources, and population. It is only natural, then, that the international struggle for power revolved around the acquisition of those goods, usually in the form of one state's stealing them from another. In today's postindustrial global economy, however, the chief source of value-added lies in technological innovation and the human capital needed to produce it.

As the example of Japan and the various city-states of Asia demonstrates, natural resources, territory, and population count for very little in the ability of a modern economy to produce tremendous amounts of wealth; what is much more important is the human capital that can be embodied in even a small labor force. And, short of physically capturing another country's scientists, that human capital cannot be created through the usual tools of statecraft. Today, the chief national interest of virtually every country in the world is a sustained level of growth in productivity and per capita income. Physical security and an open global economic system are necessary prerequisites to achieve this, but such a goal is actually *impeded* by the pursuit of power maximization in its classic form (that is, the accumulation of weapons or territory).

In the current Russian foreign policy debate, many who argue for returning to an "objective" national interest implicitly believe that this means exchanging the superpower status of the late twentieth century for the great-power status of the nineteenth. Yet today's technological, social, and economic changes mean that there are a variety of routes to great-power status and that economic might has become in many ways more important to real influence in the current international system than traditional forms of geopolitical power. National interest as a guide to foreign policy therefore dissolves like a mirage, leaving open the question: What sort of foreign policy *ought* Russia to have?

Russian "National Interest"

In discussing the nature of contemporary Russian national interest, let me begin by making a few disavowals. Having said that national interest is variable and not necessarily linked to the nationalist interests of a state's dominant ethnic group, I do *not* think it illegitimate under all circumstances for national interests to be self-interested or, indeed, nationalistic. It is absurd to think that any country can define itself as nothing other than a good global citizen, whose interests are always coterminous with the views of one or another international organization like the United Nations or the International Monetary Fund. (On the other hand, it is equally wrong to think, as some critics have charged, that the present Russian government is pursuing such a policy.) Even beyond this point, I do not think it wrong for Russia to develop an overtly nationalist foreign policy oriented primarily toward the interests of Russians, as against some of the other ethnic groups who live in Russia and are equally its citizens. If Russia does not look out for the interests of Russians, no one else will.

For while we all understand the dangers of extreme nationalism, a moderate and positive sense of national identity is both healthy in itself and necessary as the matrix within which strong national communities can be formed. It is only within the context of such national communities that democratic institutions can be established—and therefore no accident that democracy and nationalism have been closely associated since the time of the French Revolution.[4] Nations want to live for something other than consumerist prosperity and universal rights; they also want positive cultural identities and historical traditions. Since the end of World War II, most European countries have found a way of reconciling living national traditions with political tolerance and liberalism, mostly by relegating nationalism to the realm of culture and private life. All the countries of the European Community, for example, have officially condemned nationalism and set a supranational agenda for themselves, yet clearly—as opposition to the Maastricht treaty indicates—nationalism is far from dead in Western Europe. It would, needless to say, be hypocritical to assert that Russia alone should have no vital national traditions.

Sergei Stankevich argues that there are two trends in the present debate on Russian foreign policy—"Atlanticism," oriented toward the Group of Seven, or G–7, world, and "Eurasianism," oriented toward the Middle East, Asia, and the South more generally.[5] He makes a compelling argument that Russia is not now a member of the G–7 world and that it can waste a good deal of time and energy pretending to be a wealthy, first-world nation when it is not. Russia's geographic position on the borders of the Middle East and Asia, along with its Muslim-Turkic population, means that it will inevitably be more preoccupied with the affairs of that region than, say, the Caribbean. And, finally, its current economic problems are indeed similar to those being experienced by larger developing economies like those of Mexico, Brazil, and India, all of which are in the process of liberalizing and privatizing traditionally statist economies.

But whether this new home, somewhere between North and South, should be more than a transitional resting place and become a permanent domicile for Russia is quite another question. The "Eurasian" foreign policy orientation of nineteenth-century Slavophilism was based not just on Russia's geographical location, but also on the belief that Russia represented a social and political system distinctly different from that of Western Europe. If Russia's contemporary Eurasianism is premised on its retaining a political and economic system different in principle from the capitalist liberal democracy that characterizes the rest of the G–7 world, then I think it will arrive at a dead end both internally and in its foreign policy. No other development path will be capable of supporting great-power status in the twenty-first century. Mexico and Brazil, we should remember, are themselves desperate to leave the South and would be perfectly happy to be accepted someday as members of the G–7 world.

On the emotional question of Russia's "near abroad," I do not think it is at all illegitimate for a nation to be concerned with the rights and fate of its coethnics living beyond its national borders. The United States is least of all in a position to lecture other countries about this. U.S. foreign policy was obsessed for much of the past decade with the fate of a handful of its citizens held captive in Lebanon, as well as others missing earlier in the Vietnam War. Nor is the United States in a position to categorically oppose the use of force in the extraterritorial defense of its citizens. The 1983 invasion of Grenada was justified on the grounds of a threat to American medical students there, while the case for the invasion of Panama was made, to some degree, because a Panamanian National Guardsman sexually accosted the wife of a U.S. officer.

Where I disagree with Stankevich, however, is on the manner in which Russia can optimally secure the rights and dignity of those Russians outside Russia and the priority that this mission ought to have in overall Russian foreign policy. Stankevich is sensitive to the echoes and nuances of Russian history and appreciative of the constraints and obligations these place on contemporary Russians, but he is blind to similar historical legacies on the part of Russia's neighbors. Russia has a long history as an imperial and authoritarian power, and it cannot pretend that this legacy will disappear overnight. According to Stankevich,

> Contrary to all charges of an imperial syndrome, such a policy [of protecting the rights of Russians outside Russia] has nothing in common with imperialism. On the contrary, it is for Russia a legitimate and natural aspiration to the erasure of conflicts and the harmonization of relations on the territory of the former USSR, and, what is more, Russia will invariably take the part of the "undeservedly insulted and unjustly persecuted."[6]

It seems highly unlikely that the former republics should now regard a country that less than a year ago represented an imperial center as an impartial and just upholder of the "undeservedly insulted and unjustly persecuted." Stankevich characterizes those countries as being driven by "paranoid ideas of historical or national vengeance," and it is certainly true that all of them have exhibited nationalist excess. But then many paranoiacs have good reason to be afraid. Russia's transition to a postimperial democracy is very recent, and its conversion to upholding the individual rights of humankind is not of long standing. There is consequently good reason why other states should wonder whether Russian intervention on behalf of its coethnics is truly disinterested. Present-day Germany, too, has a legitimate interest in the rights of Germans outside Germany, but the legacy of Hitlerism has prevented it from promoting those rights too stridently.[7]

Stankevich dismisses "diplomatic" attempts to secure the rights of Russians abroad, but it is by no means clear that they will fail, particularly in the more European parts of the former USSR. Although there have been and will be many instances of genuine persecution of Russians abroad, in other cases—particularly in the Baltics—Russian populations are seen as fifth columns representing Russian imperial interests. Threats from Moscow on this score are likely to increase rather than decrease that suspicion.

On the other hand, Stankevich underestimates the kind of help that Russia could get from Europe and the United States in promoting principles like universal citizenship laws. Consider the Latvian draft law, which would effectively bar Latvia's many ethnic Russians from citizenship. I believe it to be a great mistake from the standpoint of long-term Latvian interests because it leaves Latvians with one of two unpalatable choices: either to deal with the political tensions created by a society in which nearly half the inhabitants are permanently disenfranchised, second-class citizens, or else to attempt to expel the latter—a truly suicidal course. On the basis of both principle and practical policy, it would seem to be incumbent on other Western democracies to support nonexclusionary citizenship laws in all of the successor states to the Soviet Union. The effect of such outside pressure on small countries like Estonia from a Europe they are eager to enter would be enormous.

The search for the best means of protecting the rights of Russians outside Russia leads, ultimately, back to Atlanticism and the G–7 world that Stankevich at least for now rejects. Given the extremely high number of Russians living outside Russia, clearly the only peaceful solution to this problem is for true liberal democracy, based on individual rights, to become institutionalized in as much of the former USSR as possible. Even if the dispute over Crimea could be solved to the satisfaction of most Russians, the rights of the Russians living in eastern Ukraine can be safeguarded only if the regime in Kiev continues to define citizenship in territorial rather than ethnic or linguistic terms and avoids policies of coercive Ukrainianization. The other alternatives to this type of liberal solution—negotiated group rights, population transfers, border adjustments, or the extraterritorial use of force to protect rights—all run a very high risk of reproducing the current situation in the former Yugoslavia within the borders of the former USSR. It is not Iran, Pakistan, or Afghanistan that will support Russian attempts to guarantee equal rights for Russians in Estonia or Ukraine, but rather the G–7 world. Atlanticism cannot therefore be neglected as a pillar of Russian foreign policy, even if Russia necessarily remains preoccupied with its "near abroad" for some time to come.

Notes

1. See Vladimir P. Lukin, "Our Security Predicament," *Foreign Policy,* no. 20 (Fall 1992): 57–75.

2. I do not necessarily mean that this is Ambassador Lukin's own view of national interest "properly understood."

3. Michael Doyle, "Kant, Liberal Legacies, and Foreign Affairs," parts 1 and 2, *Philosophy and Public Affairs* 12 (Summer, Fall 1983): 205–235, 323–353. See also his "Liberalism and World Politics," *American Political Science Review* 80 (December 1986): 1151–1169; Dean V. Babst, "A Force for Peace," *Industrial Research* 14 (April 1972): 55–58; Ze'ev Maoz and Nasrin Abdolali, "Regime Types and International Conflict, 1816–1976," *Journal of Conflict Resolution* 33 (March 1989): 3–35; and R. J. Rummel, "Libertarianism and International Violence," *Journal of Conflict Resolution* 27 (March 1983): 27–71.

4. For a positive account of contemporary nationalism in the former Soviet Union, see Ghia Nodia, "Nationalism and Democracy," *Journal of Democracy* 3, no. 4 (October 1992): 3–22.

5. Sergei B. Stankevich, *Nezavisimaia gazeta,* March 28, 1992.

6. Ibid.

7. See also Sergei B. Stankevich, *Rossiiskaia gazeta,* June 23, 1992; and *Izvestiia,* July 8, 1992.

3
Toward a New "National Idea"

Sergei B. Stankevich

Since the collapse of the Soviet Union, a debate has raged within Russia about how to define our national interests. High officials of the government, parliamentarians, distinguished experts on politics and international relations, and many others—even Americans—have taken part in this discussion. Often, of course, the debate has been nothing more than a battle of caricatures, a fight against "straw men" rather than against real arguments. Mutual misunderstanding among all the parties to the discussion has been high, and as a result the argument has been especially fierce.

Many of a country's national interests leave, in fact, almost no room for real debate. They are to a large extent predetermined by geography, history, culture, ethnic composition, and political tradition. Fundamental interests such as survival, prosperity, and security are common to all countries, and the pursuit of those interests is a natural aspect of stable international relations. The same is true of much narrower, short-term interests; these change rather frequently as a country's policies evolve to reflect changing circumstances.

Between those fundamental interests that do not change at all and those that are always changing, there is a set of interests that reflect what may be called the "national idea." The national idea is a nation's self-identity. It is a very emotional topic, one subject to the changing course of a nation's history. It is not a scientific value system but a set of visualizations of the national past—and the national future.

Very often, the carriers of the national idea are the minority, not the majority, of the population. The national idea of czarist Russia, for example, was imperial and monarchist. What mattered was "Holy Russia" and "Mother Russia." Those conceptions were abandoned, of course, after the Bolshevik Revolution. The primary elements of the new national idea became world revolution, social utopia, and the welfare state. Nevertheless, the Soviet version of Russia's national idea retained a strong imperial character, and in the course of the global confrontation of the cold war era, it became even more militarized. Then, when the confrontation came to an end, so did the interests that had been defined by it.

At present, the national idea of a new democratic Russia must be phrased with a question mark. Russia today is still moving toward a new definition of its national idea, an idea that I believe must be characterized by democracy, federalism, and patriotism. Russia must reject the imperial nature of its previous incarnations. Because it no longer has a global mission to build Communism or socialism, Russia has no reason to be involved in the so-called world revolutionary process, supporting leftist and national liberation movements in distant lands. Russia is now in a different era, where its interests are interpreted differently and formulated differently. Its interests have become, in a word, normal.

A key question in defining Russia's national interest is whether Russia will differ from the liberal democracies in any fundamental way. As I see it, Russia will retain its uniqueness, but the differences between it and other Western democracies should not be exaggerated; nor should they be considered undesirable or a sign of some irreconcilable conflict. After all, capitalism in the United States and Germany is different from capitalism in Japan and South Korea, or in Mexico and India. And the differences are not simply a matter of technological development; they reflect distinctive civilizations. Russia is a borderline civilization, floating between European and Asian forms.

Recognizing Russia's borderline status makes it easier to answer a persistent question about the orientation of its foreign policy: Will Russia follow an Atlantic policy or a Eurasian policy? This question is frequently posed as if no combination of the two were possible. A Russian foreign policy focused exclusively on the West first emerged under Peter the Great. Russia has periodically returned to this policy throughout its history, most recently under Mikhail Gorbachev and Eduard Shevardnadze, who pursued the strategy of "new thinking." A Eurasian-based foreign policy was most strongly pursued during the nineteenth century, when Russian foreign policy was characterized by isolationism from and confrontation toward Europe.

Today, neither the Atlantic nor the Eurasian orientation is, by itself, a good recipe for Russian foreign policy. Russians must seek a balance, aiming not toward integration for its own sake but toward constructive interaction. Russia in no sense rejects the idea of joining the leading states of the world. The question is, when will we enter this group and what do we have to offer the other members?

The example of twentieth-century Turkey makes clear that Russia's orientation between Europe and Asia does not have to be an exclusive one for Russia to be accepted in the West. In his attempt to define Russia's role in the world, Francis Fukuyama makes this very apt comparison: he argues that Kemal Atatürk and his followers put modernization above the interests of millions of Turkic peoples living in Iran, the Caucasus, and Soviet Central Asia and implies that this break with an imperial past can be a model for Russia.

The relevance of this model, however, depends on whether it fits the facts. Did Atatürk really reject the role of protector of Turks in the diaspora and thereby turn Turkey from an empire into a "normal" state that moved closer and closer to Western principles? In reality, Turkey's twentieth-century transformation has been far more complex. For many years, the political regime in Turkey was authoritarian in nature, with prolonged periods of military rule. This made it possible to maintain order and to avoid internal squabbling, but the reliance on force to preserve stability cannot be considered either painless or insignificant.

Equally important for our purposes, Ankara has remained especially sensitive to the problem of ethnic Turks living outside Turkey. In 1974, after all, Turkey conducted a full-scale military operation in Cyprus because, in its opinion, the interests of the Turkish community there were threatened. The consequences of that crisis are still being felt. Then, in the latter half of the 1980s, there was a flare-up of interstate tensions over the persecution of ethnic Turks in Bulgaria. Even now the situation of the Turkish minority in Bulgaria remains a matter of keen attention for Ankara. In 1992, armed incidents on the border of Nakhichevan Oblast led to warnings and troop movements by Turkey to back them up.

The disintegration of the USSR has encouraged Turkey to explore ways of strengthening its influence precisely in the region that its "European" orientation should have ruled out. In the Caucasus, in addition to Turkish diplomats and business people, one now runs into numerous "specialists in Turkic research" and advisers attached to high-ranking officials. Preparation is under way for establishing a unified banking system and a free-trade zone for all Turkic republics. At the end of October 1992, heads of the Turkic-language republics of the former USSR convened in Turkey for a national anniversary. The leaders' pilgrimage underscored their piety toward a great power that is energetically forming a new geopolitical alliance on the basis of ethnic solidarity. In July 1993, Turkey convened a meeting of the Organization for Economic Cooperation with the Central Asian states with the idea of forming a common economic union.

In all these ways, Turkey continues to advance its own geopolitical interests without hurting the tasks of its own modernization. The heirs of imperial Turkey use the factor of ethnic solidarity in their policy in a civilized manner, and no one objects to this.

Another example is Germany. Many commentators—both Russian and foreign—draw an analogy between our interest in Russians in the "near abroad" and the problem of the Sudeten Germans, who were used by the Hitler regime in the 1930s to justify German expansion. I agree that the comparison is very valuable. Not only does it provide a good historical parallel, but it clearly shows that the motives and goals of Nazi Germany and today's Russia are diametrically opposed. Germany in the late 1930s was bent on expansion; it made an imperial choice in principle and was not particularly discreet in its intentions. By contrast, Russia has made a principled *anti*-imperial choice. It does not have the slightest inclination toward expansion.

This is a significant difference. Today, when Germany takes an interest in the fate of ethnic Germans, no one invokes the Sudeten Germans or calls Hitler to mind. In October 1992, for example, the German minister of foreign affairs, Klaus Kinkel, said in Moscow that Russia's attitude toward the ethnic Germans is an issue in relations between our two states. Both Turkey and Germany consider their positions on this question to be completely "normal." So do we.

Today, Russia's main goal is to devote its full attention to its own economic problems. We must remove any obstacles that keep us from doing so. To pursue domestic economic reform, Russia needs external stability along its new borders. In addition, it is in the interest of Russian democracy to prevent potential expansionists and opponents of political reform from using events beyond our borders to weaken the new democratic regime.

The civic equality of ethnic Russians abroad is a normal national interest for Russia, but the problem is unique in its seriousness and its scale. It involves the fate of 25 million people. Obviously, intervention on their behalf can be used as a pretext for territorial expansion, but this is not Russia's purpose. That route would be fraught with dangerous consequences for everyone. Diplomatic measures are a must—and must not be merely a show, a disguise or pretext for flexing our muscles, much less for new discrimination or ethnic cleansing.

Russia must defend its interests in anti-imperialist ways. What is at stake is our internal stability. Unless we resolve this problem, it will remain a constant source of tension that could explode at any time.

All these reasons give Russia the strongest concrete interest in reducing tensions among the states of the former USSR. The same interest in a favorable geopolitical climate is not shared by all those states, however. In Estonia and Latvia, for example, where other ideas prevail, one gets the impression that some politicians are interested in whipping up the tensions surrounding the ethnic Russians who live there. For unsuccessful reformers, nationalist propaganda is the easiest and cheapest way to mobilize domestic political support. By claiming to be a Western buffer against Russia's "aggressive designs," these aspiring architects of a Baltic cordon sanitaire are hoping to win long-term, substantial aid from the Atlantic community and a number of northern European countries.

To enhance the significance of the Baltic border and to gain additional geopolitical weight, some Baltic politicians have spoken of a gradual rapprochement with the North Atlantic Treaty Organization. This talk has not ruled out the creation of joint military units whose task would be to fill the vacuum left by the withdrawal of Russian troops. Such a turn of events could hardly be accepted painlessly by Russia. It will regard any steps toward the cordon sanitaire concept as unfriendly and provocative.

It is sometimes said that Russia, in its dealings with other states of the former Soviet Union, must atone for an imperialist past. Accordingly, Russia must be sensitive to the feelings of those who regard it as their former imperial master. This is Fukuyama's position, and many others have expressed the same view. But we must be clear in our analysis: Which Russia are we talking about?

It was neither Russia nor the Russians that sent troops into the Baltics in 1940, into Hungary in 1956, into Czechoslovakia in 1968, and into Afghanistan in 1979. It was the ruling elite of the totalitarian Soviet state that pursued those actions. Russia did not occupy other countries or impose anything on them. In fact, of all the republics of the former Union, Russia itself sustained the greatest human and material losses during the years of "socialist development."

It was Russia that took upon itself the main burden of the struggle against totalitarianism and for democratic change. It was, again, Russia that assumed the main burden of bringing order to the post-Soviet legacy. Among other things, it was Russia that took the lead in the withdrawal and rebilleting of troops. It is Russia that has sought to resolve numerous conflicts in the republics of the former USSR. Finally, the citizens of the newly independent states must remember that it is only because democracy now prevails in Russia that they too are able to enjoy democracy.

Attempts to blame Russia or Russians for the crimes of the Soviet Union are the result of malicious lies and historic blindness. Today's Russia and Russians are no more responsible for the deeds of Soviet leaders than today's Latvia and its citizens are for the deeds of thousands of Latvian riflemen on Russian soil in 1917. Nothing done in the past can justify hasty anti-Russian actions such as the obvious discrimination against a million and a half ethnic Russians in Estonia and Lithuania. The situation in the Baltics is most dangerous, because it is here in the heart of Europe that modern apartheid has been enacted as law.

There is a certain bitter irony in the fact that ethnic Russians, the majority of whom supported Estonian and Latvian independence and were ready to become loyal citizens, have instead become victims of this movement. How is it possible to justify a situation in which a person born in Estonia, whose children were born in Estonia, suddenly loses the right to be an Estonian citizen? Russians in both Estonia and Latvia voted in parliamentary elections that proclaimed independence and participated in referendums relating to independence. Now it turns out that they were needed only by the zealots of national democracy. They were "disposable" citizens.

From across the ocean, Fukuyama reminds us that if Russia does not take care of the interests of Russians, no one else will. One might think no one could argue with such a statement. Surprisingly, there are many in Russia who do. According to them, if a former native of Russia does not have a stamp of Russian citizenship in his passport, only the international community can protect him; Russia cannot. Unfortunately, the international community has expressed no desire to offer such protection.

The attempts of some Western leaders to demonstrate their "understanding" of discriminatory actions by Estonian and Latvian authorities are an affront to international law and common sense. It is outrageous that they are willing to condone the barring of 40 percent of Estonia's residents from participating in the elections or the consigning of Russians born in Estonia and Latvia (frequently over two generations) as foreigners subject to naturalization. Russia simply cannot accept such limitations on the rights of Russians living abroad. Against this background, Fukuyama's view that the current Estonian citizenship policy leads either to apartheid or to "ethnic cleansing"—but is in any case suicidal—is unquestionably realistic.

Nevertheless, there is no reason to think that the Group of Seven nations (G–7) will render effective assistance to Russia in protecting the legitimate rights of ethnic minorities in the territory of the former USSR. To judge by the weak reaction to the "ethnically cleansed" Estonian elections, nothing will be done beyond symbolic gestures of little significance. For instance, in the September 1992 report "Russians in Estonia: Problems and Prospects," the Commission on Security and Cooperation in Europe of the U.S. Congress justified barring ethnic Russians from elections because these "deprived people," according to some public opinion surveys, are more concerned with their economic situation and property issues than with elections. The implication is appallingly clear: if the economy is your main concern, you have no business taking part in elections.

The authors of the report also placed the responsibility for the potential worsening of inter-ethnic relations in Estonia squarely on the shoulders of politicians in Moscow. The authors believe that, by calling attention to injustice in the Baltics, Russian politicians may destroy the emerging democratic movement. Once again, the

West has failed to focus on the primary issue of human rights in the Baltics.

Those who count on the leaders of Western democracies to protect the rights of Russian ethnic minorities in the republics of the former USSR will be disappointed. In the worst-case scenario, everything the former Soviet republics do against the bearer of the "imperial threat" will be automatically justified. In the best-case scenario, Western governments will avoid the controversial topic and, by their silence, condone the emergence of apartheid in places like the Baltics. The failure of the West to respond is clear; it is simply naive to expect anything different in the future. Russia cannot accept the discrimination currently practiced in Estonia and is perfectly prepared to work alone to resolve the situation.

Those who say Russia's history will keep it from acting as a force for reconciliation among different peoples fail to recognize the fundamental transformation that has occurred in Russia during the past two years. In particular, Russia's role as a peacemaking and peacekeeping force has become evident. Consider the case of Moldova. The involvement of the United Nations and then the Conference on Security and Cooperation in Europe in the Trans-Dniester conflict ended in failure. By contrast, Russian diplomacy brought temporary stabilization. In the future, only Russian diplomacy will lead to long-term stabilization in the area.

Russia has also sought a formula for reconciliation in the conflict in Georgia, South Ossetia, and Abkhazia. And after many months of internal conflict, Tajikistan turned to Russia to mediate between warring parties. Russia is the only country capable of resolving the instability in the region. Russia's ability to promote conciliation has been demonstrated during these particular conflicts. Russia must seek to play a vital unifying and conciliatory role among the former Soviet republics. This role of mediator of regional conflicts is becoming an important aspect of the Russian national idea.

Let me sum up: Russia today is capable of effectively securing its own national interests. These interests at present incorporate the following principles: self-preservation; prevention of further collapse; creation of a system of democracy and federalism that checks both imperial dictatorship and separatist tendencies; efficient guarantees for ethnic Russians who live in the "near abroad";

and the evolution of a strong and efficient state with a stable foreign policy.

These national interests for Russia are like those of great powers everywhere. And they are more than that. They reflect the
country's natural needs as well as the fundamental transformation
brought to Russia by its democratic revolution.

4

Russia, Ukraine, and Eastern Europe

Nikolai Travkin

The collapse of Communist regimes in Eastern Europe has destroyed the seemingly inflexible matrix of relationships that developed during the cold war. The end of the USSR in December 1991 and the emergence of 15 independent states in its place further complicate the situation. And yet the spirit of the Soviet Union continues to influence events around the world. The new leaders of Eastern Europe remain haunted by the ghosts of history. In other countries, people continue to accuse Russia of aggressive and imperialistic designs, ascribing to it the past sins of the USSR. These suspicions and fears are fueled by irresponsible politicians both inside and outside Russia. Russia, it seems, has become a crutch for those who cannot explain the failure of their own reform efforts.

Although much was achieved as a result, the rapid liquidation of the USSR was a fundamental mistake. The gradual transformation of existing political and economic structures to a more equitable system that recognized the independence and sovereignty of the former republics of the Soviet Union would have been a more rational and fruitful approach. Instead, the economic system has been thrown into disarray, and the standard of living throughout the former Union has plummeted. The political system swings perilously from chaos to gridlock. Military discipline and organizational control on the territory of the former Soviet Union have broken down. As a result, the entire area, from Brest-Litovsk to Vladivostok, from Murmansk to Dushanbe, is a giant tinderbox that could ignite at any moment.

Russia and the Commonwealth of Independent States

The traditional structure of Russia's foreign policy, both economic and political, has been fundamentally redefined since 1991. Historically, Russia's national interests and foreign relations have formed concentric circles. The first and innermost circle was reserved for the republics of the Soviet Union, with their integrated economies and transparent political borders. The countries of the socialist camp filled the second circle; geographical borders in this circle were more concrete, but politically and economically these countries were still closely integrated. The Western democracies, viewed with suspicion and mistrust, formed the final foreign policy circle in the framework.

The collapse of the Soviet Union changed this arrangement. The Russian foreign ministry and the Russian government initiated a hasty policy of realignment, catering primarily to the interests of the United States and Western Europe but to the detriment of Russia's geopolitical and domestic interests. Based on unrealistically high expectations for Western assistance, the Russian leadership anticipated a quick and efficient solution to Russia's problems. After many months of exceedingly difficult economic, political, and social trials, however, it is clear Russia must rely on itself to end the crises it faces.

The most important element of Russia's new foreign policy must be the development of relations with countries of the Commonwealth of Independent States (CIS). These countries are inextricably linked by geographical proximity and historical ties. In addition, the last 70 years have established an integrated common market that must be maintained. Western Europe has been trying for decades to create one, and Russia cannot afford to lose its own to the whims and ambitions of regional leaders.

In its relations with the newly independent countries of the former Soviet Union, Russia's primary mission is to provide leadership in restoring regional integration. Currently, this leadership role has been assumed by Kazakhstan's president, Nursultan Nazarbayev. The Soviet breakup has severed many ties based on common strategic, social, political, and economic needs. What is needed now is not the reconstruction of the Soviet Union but, instead, the restoration of some of those beneficial ties. Integration cannot be forced on the countries of the former Soviet Union. Only a rational assessment of, and respect for, the needs of each country can lead to the reintegration of the region.

Integration among the countries of the former USSR would be mutually beneficial to all countries involved. The establishment of a common economic structure, for example, would ease economic reform in the area. Uniform citizenship laws could guarantee that human rights are observed on an equal basis. A coordinated foreign policy would increase the collective influence of the countries in world affairs. Finally, the establishment of unified armed forces would greatly ease the burden of maintaining small, independent defenses.

Because it is the only nation capable of serving as the focus of this new union, Russia must assume the leadership in this effort. Only Russia can assume the role of protector and guarantor for the smaller states of the former Union. In addition, it is through such a union that Russia can best support Russians who now find themselves living in foreign countries.

Developing a viable economic union must be the principal goal of developing close relations among the countries of the CIS. The European Community can serve as a model for the political framework of this new confederation. Conducting a strategy of joint economic reforms, this union can pursue cooperative monetary and fiscal policies. Agreements on prices and tariffs are necessary to support such a union, because an immediate switch to world prices would mean an economic collapse for all countries involved and an even sharper decline of living standards. The structure created should also provide for the free movement of capital, labor resources, commodities, and services.

The development of this union would certainly require the following: creation of interstate economic institutions; an arbitration court; a system of sanctions for violations of agreements; the systematic harmonization of legislation that regulates economic activities on the territories of all member-states; the establishment of large-scale benefits for creating integrated commercial structures; investments in the development of an interstate market infrastructure; and the development and implementation of large-scale joint projects with imported technologies and capital.

While it works to integrate the economies of the region, Russia must actively prevent the rise of ethnic conflict, because any violence will directly affect the situation inside Russia. This fact must be clearly understood in formulating Russia's national interests. Its military presence in the region makes it necessary for Russia to assume this role. At the same time, the history of Russian involvement in the region precludes actual military involvement. Therefore, Russia must actively pursue a policy that seeks to resolve ethnic conflict *before* it leads to bloodshed.

Relations with Ukraine

Among the countries of the CIS, Russian foreign policy must focus on Ukraine. Russia must develop a specific plan, based on complete respect for Ukrainian independence and sovereignty. Such a policy is necessary not only because Ukraine is Russia's chief economic partner and the second most populous CIS country, but also because the Russian people and their historical memory demand that a priority be placed on Ukrainian relations. For Russia and Ukraine alike, Kiev is our common home, the source of our common language, common religion, and common culture. We share a common value system. Every Russian understands these fundamental facts. No matter how history proceeds—how presidents and parliaments behave—a Ukrainian will always be a Russian's closest friend. In the development of Russia's foreign policy, then, these cultural considerations must stand on an equal footing with economic principles.

History requires that Russia's relations with Ukraine be qualitatively different from its relations with other foreign countries. Russia must understand the Ukrainian peoples' desire to assert their identity and must provide Ukraine with whatever assistance possible. Russia should also be prepared to make numerous concessions. In time, this policy will be justified through the goodwill of Russia's neighbors and friends. It is important to remember that the future of the Ukrainian-Russian relationship is more important than any current disagreements.

Today's euphoria of independence in Ukraine has led many Ukrainian politicians to call for a rupture of all ties with Russia. Many press for Ukraine's full reorientation toward the West. These feelings are at times fueled by Ukraine's current leaders to divert public attention from their inability to ease the country's domestic problems. For example, a Ukrainian spokesman once blamed former Russian prime minister Egor Gaidar and the Russian government—not Ukrainian president Leonid Kravchuk—for the failure of reform in Ukraine.

The collapse of the USSR, which was the product of the ambitions of politicians in Moscow and Kiev, ruptured many beneficial ties and has depressed both Russia's and Ukraine's living standards. Ukraine has suffered even more than Russia. We in Russia hope that reason will triumph in Ukraine sooner or later and that the country will realize that broad-based cooperation with Russia is the key to future development. Meanwhile, Russia's Ministry of Foreign Affairs continues to pay insufficient attention to Ukraine. The Russian government, too, must realize that Russia's future development is predicated on closer relations with Kiev.

Following the formation of the CIS, the Ukrainian nationalist movement *Rukh* supported Kravchuk and abandoned its democratic program in favor of striving for national independence. Contacts between Russian and Ukrainian parties nearly ended as *Rukh* pursued an active anti-Russia policy, demanding an immediate, and complete, break with Russia. Part of that anti-Russia policy included attempts to destroy the Russian Federation; *Rukh* delegations were sent to the Kuban and Tatarstan in support of local separatist movements.

Now, however, economic reform and its difficulties have sobered many of the supporters of complete and immediate independence. The position of the extremely nationalistic *Rukh* wing led by Vyacheslav Chornovil has clearly failed to get nationwide support. Instead, more pragmatic movements such as *Novaya Ukraina* have been steadily gaining ground, primarily because their focus is on economic problems. These parties have toned down the anti-Russia tenor of recent Ukrainian political debate. In the beginning of summer 1992, Russia and Ukraine saw a nearly simultaneous birth of influential political blocs—the Civic Union in Russia and Ukraine's Civic Congress—favoring the transformation of the CIS into a confederation. From the start, these organizations established contact with each other.

A long-term and stable national policy must be based on the interests of broad sections of society and on the parties and movements that represent those interests. Relations between Ukraine and Russia will largely be determined by the positions and relationships of the political organizations of the two countries.

Overall, developments warrant the hope that nations and political organizations will outpace their governments in their progress

toward rapprochement. A close and advantageous alliance between Russia and Ukraine is inevitable. It is the responsibility of
the Ukrainian and Russian governments to respond to public senti-
ment in the development of this relationship.

Relations with Eastern Europe

The collapse of the USSR has had an equally unsettling impact on
the countries of what had come to be known as Eastern Europe.
This region is now struggling through a difficult transition from the
cold war to the "new world order." Under the old order, the Warsaw Pact countries enjoyed nominal independence. However,
many of them are just now coming to understand the reality of true
independence. They have embarked on the search for their own
national interests. This transformation of values has begun while
the old system has not been completely dismantled and the new
one has yet to take shape.

The destruction of the Eastern market hit all its players hard.
Despite calls for integration with the West, the Western markets no
longer have vacant niches. The restoration of the Eastern market
and its development are imperative for the economic reform of the
entire region. Russia's economic interests would be well served by
a preferential protectionist policy that would enable East European
countries to trade their noncompetitive products for Russian noncompetitive products. It is incumbent on the Russian government
to develop a foreign policy that reflects this fundamental objective—the creation of an Eastern market.

Poland. As with many countries in Eastern Europe, Russia's relations with Poland are complicated by the past. In the nineteenth
century, much of Poland was annexed by Imperial Russia. In the
twentieth century, the 1939 Hitler-Stalin pact divided Poland between Nazi Germany and the USSR. In 1940, several thousand captive Polish officers were executed in the Katyn forest near
Smolensk. In the 1980s, the USSR encouraged and supported the
suppression of the trade union Solidarity.

Polish animosity over past Soviet outrages did not disappear
with the disappearance of the Soviet Union. Polish relations with
Russia remained cool. Nevertheless, many Polish intellectuals and
leaders of the Polish democratic movement never equated the

USSR's imperial policy with the Russians and Russia; these people have always favored cooperation. Statements in this vein have been made repeatedly in interviews with the Russian press by Adam Michnik, one of the founding fathers of Solidarity. Poland's president Lech Walesa was able to make a successful visit to Russia in May 1992, signing a troop pullout treaty that eliminated the main stumbling block in relations between Moscow and Warsaw. Gradually, the Polish attitude toward Russia has been changing.

Bulgaria. Historically and culturally, Russia has closer ties with Bulgaria than with any of its other East European neighbors. The Russians and the Bulgarians share a common alphabet, religion, and cultural tradition. For centuries Russia fought against Turkish domination of Bulgaria and for Bulgaria's independence.

Yet relations between these countries have had a checkered history. During World War II, Bulgaria sided with Nazi Germany, and after the war the USSR installed a Communist regime in Sofia. Thus, after the breakup of the USSR, Russia was viewed with suspicion. These suspicions were largely dispelled after Boris Yeltsin became the first European leader to recognize Macedonia while visiting Sofia on August 6, 1992. In addition, Russia's support for Bulgaria's position on Macedonia helped Bulgaria greatly in the international arena.

Economically, Bulgaria's ties with Russia were the strongest within the Council for Mutual Economic Assistance (COMECON). In the future, Bulgaria will certainly seek a more balanced foreign economic policy, but for objective reasons Russia will remain Bulgaria's chief economic and political partner.

Hungary. Like Bulgaria, Hungary's history of relations with Russia has seen its ups and downs. In 1848, the Russian Army suppressed the Hungarian revolution; during World War II, Hungary was among the most loyal of Hitler's allies; in 1956, Nikita Khrushchev sent troops into Hungary to restore a Communist regime there.

Today, Russia has good relations with Hungary, with a formidable potential for development. The biggest potential difference between Russia and Hungary is in their respective policies toward the fate of the former Yugoslavia. Hungary has traditionally supported Croatia, while Russia backs its Slavic comrades.

Despite these difficulties, Hungary and Russia have much in common. In addition to the economic ties common to all the nations of the extinct COMECON, Hungary's diaspora is second in size only to Russia's among European nations. (The Hungarians live in Transylvania, Romania; Vojvodina, Serbia; and Slovenia.) As a result, the Hungarian leadership has empathetic feelings for the problems of divided nations and seeks to promote the rights of ethnic minorities.

Czechoslovakia. Russia's relations with Czechoslovakia (although regrettably tarnished by the Soviet invasion of 1968) have always been amicable. The breakup of Czechoslovakia into the Czech Republic and Slovakia, however, upset the formerly unified country's system of relations with the outside world. Still, both the nationalists in Slovakia and the pro-Western leaders in the Czech Republic have a stake in preserving close ties with Russia to stabilize their economic and political situations. Russia has no conflicts with either nation and will seek to develop cooperation with both, without giving preference to either.

Romania. Moldova will remain the largest stumbling block in relations between Russia and Romania. Sadly, the Romanian leadership has supported Kishinev's adventurist policy, which seeks the destruction of the Trans-Dniestr Republic. This policy has claimed hundreds of human lives. The present government in Romania is more moderate than some of the opposition forces. If, however, the opposition gains greater influence over Romania's foreign policy, relations with Russia will hardly be improved.

Nevertheless, Russia is willing to develop economic and political relationships with Romania both on a bilateral basis and within the framework of the Black Sea process launched at the Istanbul summit.

Yugoslavia. The situation in the former Yugoslavia is the thorniest problem in Europe today. It shows that Europe will bow to German pressure, supporting Germany's traditional policy aimed at the division of Yugoslavia and the support of Croatia against Serbia. It is sad that today's Russian leadership, in particular the Foreign Ministry, sees eye-to-eye with Germany, ignoring Russian interests.

Mindful of its traditional ties with Serbia, Russia cannot side with either party in the former Yugoslavia but instead should pursue an unbiased policy recognizing that all parties are equally responsible for the conflict. Russia should favor sanctions against both Serbia and Croatia.

Conclusion

Before the failed August coup of 1991, the acquisition of political power in the Soviet Union was not seen as a realistic goal for democrats opposed to the Communist Party. As a result, the destruction of the USSR as a political and economic union became the focus of democratic forces. In pursuit of this program, Russia's democrats joined nationalist forces at the Kharkov congress of January 1991. The development of this policy placed the rights of nations above those of individuals. It was the pursuit of these policies by Russian and Ukrainian democrats that was largely responsible for the collapse of the Soviet Union.

Since then, Russia's foreign policy has continued to pursue unwise and unrealistic goals. A "sobering-up" should take place in the near future, however. The pressure of reality and demands from below will lead to the development of a policy along the lines set forth here. The euphoria of sovereignty will fade and in fact has already begun to lose its luster. The high ratings initially given to those who promised rapid changes are evaporating. More reasonable and sober-minded political forces are gaining strength.

Today, the prospects for the development of Russia's relations with the countries of Eastern Europe and the other former Soviet states are very promising. Development in the right direction will be promoted by the traditions of cooperation and assistance that originated well before the Communist period. Furthermore, the real needs of the region's economies, dependent on one another for 45 years, will necessitate this change. Russian raw materials and the Russian market will always be attractive to the countries of the CIS and Eastern Europe. Similarly, Russia will need the markets of those countries for its exports. Once the euphoria of independence has passed, the newly independent countries of Eastern Europe and the former Soviet Union will realize that only a coordinated economic policy will lead to future growth.

5
Russia as a Eurasian Power: Moscow and the Post-Soviet Successor States

Paul A. Goble

After a long history of submersion in broader political entities, Russia is back—a welcome development for Russia, her immediate neighbors, and the entire world. But this transition is in every way as traumatic in the short term as that submersion, because it requires a fundamental redefinition of past identities and relationships. Nowhere is this task more complicated and difficult than in the case of Moscow's evolving relationship with the 14 non-Russian successor states that emerged alongside it following the demise of the Soviet Union. And nowhere is it more important, because progress in these relations will have a profound impact on Russia itself and on its relations with other countries as well. Consequently, I want to examine this task in some detail.

To do so, I have divided my essay into three parts. In the first, I consider the shift, particularly difficult for Russia, from a mission-oriented foreign policy to an interest-driven one and the implications of that shift for both Russia and the new countries surrounding it. In the second, I examine in a more cursory fashion the real and legitimate interests that Russia has in these states. And in the third, I explore the ways in which these interests can be effectively pursued and those in which these and even broader interests will be subverted. I have organized my essay in this way because I am convinced that if Russia and its elites can make this psychological shift, Russia will be on the road to economic revival and democratic reform, but that if they cannot, no amount of economic reforms or political activity will save the situation.

A Country Like No Other

No idea is more central in Russian history than that Russia cannot be measured in the same way as other states, that Russia has a special mission in the world and a new word by which to describe it. For much of Russian history, that word was linked to Russian

Orthodoxy and the ideas of the Third Rome. It was then transformed into the Marxist vision that Russia could represent a special way to the future. More recently, it has been suggested that Russia has a special role to play in bringing democracy and free-market capitalism to the 14 non-Russian successor states.

Such an approach has been particularly attractive to the Russian intelligentsia and the Russian state. The idea of mission is grand, systematic, and redolent of being the proper task of a great power and thus starkly in contrast to the grubby and petty questions of interest, questions that could concern only small countries and small minds. Moreover, it is exclusive and beyond compromise: it can only be pursued regardless of cost and not compromised regardless of gain. And it implies that the bearers are elevated in their task beyond the commonplace.

Such convictions are not unique to Russia. Indeed, it could be argued that the United States and Russia have shared this approach, if not its specific content. Neither the United States nor Russia has been a European power, and both have talked far more about mission than about interests. Now that the cold war is over, however, both are having to shift gears, to reckon with a diminished position in the world and, more frighteningly, to come to terms with the fact that their roles will be defined more by a calculation of interests than by a pursuit of mission. Not surprisingly, many in both countries are undergoing acute withdrawal pains from the loss of their missionary role and are engaging in both massive denial and a search for enemies that will justify remaining with the old conception.

To say all this is not to imply that either the United States or Russia only pursued a mission, that they were *causes* instead of *countries* in every case. Great powers and great peoples need a sense that they are doing something out of the ordinary in their involvement with the world. Russia has certainly needed this sense and needs it now, but the end of the cold war provides a useful time to look at the dangers of a single-minded pursuit of mission. The virtues of behaving more like European states that have long been associated with a more interest-driven foreign policy are also useful to examine lest either Russia or the United States continues to sacrifice much of its treasure and prospects in a struggle without limits.

Russia's shift from mission to interest will be particularly difficult in the case of its dealings with the non-Russian successor states for three reasons. First, the tragedy of Russia is that it became an empire long before it consolidated as a nation. It thus was a state with a center and periphery but not a metropole with colonies. As a result, the psychological boundaries of Russia are even more ambiguous than its physical ones, and many Russians are finding it difficult to live with what they consider their own country being under "foreign" rule. Second, this tragedy is compounded by the very real problems connected with the presence of more than 25 million Russians in the successor states and by the physical presence there of numerous Russian-built institutions of all kinds. And third, the shift is made additionally difficult by the psychological disposition of the leaders of the successor states to blame Russia and Russians for what were, in fact, Soviet actions and to thus act in ways that necessarily alienate all the groups involved.

As will be seen below, Russia has very real interests in these countries, interests that will be deemed legitimate by both the successor states and the world community. To date, however, Russia and Russians have talked more about loss and about mission than about those interests. The nostalgia for the USSR that is growing in Russia, the fear that the successor states will either collapse into violence that could spread to Russia or become *places d'armes* for countries hostile to Russia, the sense that all current problems are traceable to the collapse of the old system rather than to the features of that system—all these things are giving an ever bigger audience to those who want to talk in terms of mission.

But it is precisely such talk that will make it impossible for Russia to live at peace with its neighbors, to develop as a democracy, and to achieve integration into the West. Missionary zeal simply breeds resentment and thus becomes a self-fulfilling prophecy about ingratitude. Consequently, of all Russia's tasks, thinking about interests is the most immediate: if Russia can articulate its interests, their pursuit will be seen as more just than if it insists on carrying out a mission.

Yet another complicating factor in this traumatic shift is the highly differentiated nature of Russia's new neighbors. Some to the west are relatively stable and moving along the paths of nation-building and state-building; others to the south and east are already descending into chaos. Obviously the latter receive the greatest attention because they spark the greatest fears, but to the extent that this leads anyone in Moscow to conclude that a common approach will work for all, allow me to recall the following fundamental principle of political life: Equal policies applied in inherently unequal situations necessarily produce unequal and unanticipated results that can be sustained only at the price of the use of more coercion than a more differentiated approach allows. That is the trap that the Soviet Union under Mikhail Gorbachev fell into; it is a trap that can only be avoided if there is precise calculation of interests rather than the articulation of a general mission.

Russia's Real and Legitimate Interests

To say that Russia should follow the example of Europe and use interests rather than mission as a basis of its foreign policy is not to say all that much. Interests must be defined, they must vary over time as situations change, and they must be articulated in a way that generates political support. Obviously, in a culture where mission has dominated interests for a long time, that is not going to be easy. The U.S. administration is finding it extremely difficult just now, and we should expect Russia to find it no easier. Moreover, interests are the product of the political system and its place in the psychological world of its population. Thus, it is in some ways totally inappropriate for outsiders to say what Russia's interests are: we can only suggest how those interests appear to us and thus create a benchmark of probable reaction to any actions based on them. It would be immodest to claim any more, whether with regard to Moscow's relations with the successor states or to its ties to the East or West more generally.

Nonetheless, several things are clear in the area of Moscow's relations with the successor states. Both the Russian state and Russian society have certain obvious economic, political, and security interests in those countries, interests that are very specific and defensible. Let us consider each in turn.

Russia's *economic interests* are obvious: Russian industry needs access to ports, raw materials, transport and communication facilities, currency exchange, labor, and other goods in these countries. Some of these interests reside with the state, but an increasing number reside with the society. Thus Moscow will have a compelling interest to ensure access to transport and communication facilities, and it has important leverage to achieve this given its own economic interlinkage with the economies of these states. But fortunately, the successor states have an almost equally compelling interest in remaining in these linkages: none of them wanted autarky or a complete divorce from Russian economic institutions, as Gorbachev falsely proclaimed throughout his failed tenure.

At the same time, Russia's interests in economic questions are highly differentiated. The Baltic ports are probably more significant than natural resources in Turkmenistan to Russian development, and the question of airspace over Belarus is more critical than the same question where Kyrgyzstan is concerned. Consequently, Russian interests need to be expressed extremely specifically, both so they will be acceptable to others and so that Russia itself will understand that its relations with these new countries are just that—relations with new countries.

Russia's *political interests* are even more impressive, if often more frightening to the surrounding states. Russia has a clear interest in cooperation with virtually all of the successor states on a variety of political questions, again in a highly differentiated manner, and this interest cannot and should not be denied by others. Russia's interest in its citizens abroad is a natural consular function, but its concern about the fate of its coethnics abroad is more complicated and difficult and requires special comment.

By 1988, Gorbachev was insisting that the Soviet Union could not be allowed to fail because more than 60 million of its inhabitants lived outside their own ethnic territories. Now, many in Russia insist on a special Russian role in all the new states because there are 25 million Russians living outside the Russian Federation. This is an entirely legitimate concern. The new states have adopted a variety of approaches, some good, some not, and Moscow has a special right to be concerned about the fate of Russians abroad. That is not an issue; the issue, as we shall see, is the manner in which that interest is prosecuted, because if it is prosecuted in certain ways—via the use of military force, for example—the ends of protecting and integrating Russians in these new states will be subverted by the means.

But beyond this issue, Russia has an obvious political interest in playing a special role in all these new countries, in working together with them and in coordinating policies. Most of the elites of the new countries admit this in private, but they find it difficult to do so in public precisely because they are new countries, with newly assertive elites demanding a more reactive approach. Russia is the only state with a large and articulated bureaucracy and a long tradition of not being dominated by another power. As a result, it is in a good position to engage in such political dialogue, but its very preparations to do so may appear threatening.

Russia's *security interests,* the third leg of this stool, are the most important and the most difficult to specify from the outside. There are at least three different issues here.

First, Russia has a compelling interest in making sure that instability in the Caucasus and Central Asia does not expand, luring in outside powers and spilling over into Russia itself. Moscow's recent efforts to work out some form of peacekeeping through the Commonwealth of Independent States (CIS) are commendable, if perhaps on occasion counterproductive, precisely because from the perspective of some groups Russian peacekeeping looks very much like Russian projection of imperial power. Indeed, if carefully articulated, Russian interests will find broad support because few people have any interest in generating more "great games" between East and West or between North and South.

Second, Russia has an even more compelling interest in making sure that no outside power hostile to it exploits instability to establish a *place d'armes* in a nearby and weak state. Most states outside the boundaries of the former Soviet Union appear to understand this—that any projection of military power into Central Asia or the Baltics would be counterproductive, generating a Russian response or otherwise subverting common interests in peace and stability. Indeed, moves to keep outside powers out, particularly those intending to subvert the independence of the new states, are likely to be accepted by most Western leaders; after all, the greatest danger in the post–cold war world is that small conflicts will draw in too many outside powers and then explode into conflicts that cannot be managed. The United Nations, with full Russian participation, has already played a useful role in this connection; but its utility has been greatest when the power deployed is in no way related to the specific interests of a specific country.

Third, Russia has certain specific interests in particular military sites, at least for a transitional period. The Skrunda radar station in Latvia may be one example; naval access through Ukraine may be another. Such military assets, of course, change their value over time, with some sites losing all importance and others that had been of negligible interest becoming increasingly valuable. Again, it is very difficult to predict, but a definition of interests that denies that there are changes is necessarily counterproductive.

The Difficult Pursuit of Interests

One reason that many Russians as well as others are clinging to a sense of mission rather than shifting to a calculation of interests is that the pursuit of interests is probably even more difficult than their definition. Missions can be pursued regardless of cost, overriding any objections; interests must be pursued on a cost-benefit basis, with compromises and corrections constant features of political life. Moreover, and more to the point here, the pursuit of a mission appears noble regardless of method, while the pursuit of interests appears somehow selfish and can often be counterproductive to the achievement of those interests.

This interactive quality between ends and means, between interests and the methods used to pursue them, is particularly evident in Russia's difficult relationships with the new successor states. In sharp contrast to the recent past, Moscow's actions in the new countries around it frequently have been counterproductive and have generated the very things that they sought to avoid. Indeed, the shift from domestic to international politics in this old relationship has been especially difficult for Moscow because Russia is no longer in a position to simply insist on particular points, or at least on all of them all of the time. Instead, it has to balance the costs of doing certain things with the benefits to be achieved—and that is hard for those who still think that the Soviet arrangement has some kind of future.

One could consider many different cases of this: I would like to focus on only three—the use of the Commonwealth of Independent States as a means for projecting Russian power, the notion that the 14 successor states should be discussed as the "near abroad," and the use of Russian military assets in the new countries to prosecute Russian non-military goals.

As things stand now, the CIS can go in any one of three directions. It can disintegrate as more states follow Ukraine's lead in opting out of most of its discussions. It can become a true commonwealth where all the participants see that they have a stake in its continuance. Or it can be simply an expression of Russian power, a means to reassert Russian control over the periphery. The third option, however, contains within it the seeds of its own, and perhaps Russia's, destruction. If Moscow tries to reassert its control this way, either it will have to put up with ever more states leaving, perhaps with only a Russian-Turkic core remaining, or it will have to invest so much in military force that it will find its own democratic development foreclosed. No one should forget that the integration of Western Europe in the European Community was possible only because it was slow and unforced. Had the Treaty of Maastricht been proposed in the 1950s, not even an Iron and Steel Community would have been created. That is the lesson Gorbachev did not learn in his efforts to rewrite the Union treaty; it is a lesson about the need to understand that in politics, timing is everything.

Even more self-subverting are the discussions about the "near abroad" and the notion that the 14 successor states should be dealt with not via the Foreign Ministry but through a special ministry of their own. It should be obvious that the prosecution of Russian interests in this way will inevitably undermine those interests. None of the successor states, not even the most pliant in Central Asia, could accept such a diminution of their international standing and survive. And all are virtually certain to see in these increasingly frequent discussions in Moscow not an articulation of legitimate Russian interests but rather a reapportionment of Russian power that must be resisted. In short, these ideas carry within themselves the seeds of their own destruction or of the destruction of Russian democracy itself. Anyone who wants to see Russia flourish as a democracy and a free-market power needs to recognize that such apparent Russian interests are entirely false.

Concerning the use of Russian military assets, the danger of interests being subverted by their pursuit is nowhere more in evidence than in suggestions that there should be a clear linkage between Russian military withdrawal from the successor states and the treatment of Russian minorities in these new countries. A first glance might suggest that unless Moscow uses its military dominance to protect these Russians—citizens or otherwise—it will never be able to protect them politically. But such an argument is deeply flawed, precisely because this linkage prevents either the Russian communities abroad or their host states and societies from coming to terms with the new reality of independence. To the extent that the Russians are seen as only an adjunct to the Russian army, no host government can afford to be generous in dealing with them—at least once the force itself is gone.

The entire world has a vested interest in seeing that the human rights of all minorities—Russian and non-Russian alike—are protected. The use of military power and military rhetoric to do so, however, recalls the 1930s, when such linkage led to war. But the danger to Russia from such an approach is even greater in three respects. First, the use of military power to "solve" political problems will undermine democratic development in Russia itself by expanding the role of the military at a time when it should be contracting for the benefit of Russian society. Second, to be effective, such use would have to continue for a very long time and is therefore likely to give rise to conflicts that we cannot even anticipate. And third, it could ultimately work to Russia's disadvantage in yet another way.

In Vladimir Nabokov's classic novel *Pnin,* the hero, in one of his celebrated mixed metaphors, remarks: "People who live in glass houses should not try to kill two birds with one stone." Russia faces serious ethnic and political challenges at home. It is not the Soviet Union writ small and need not suffer the same end. But a policy of force in the successor states and a continuing attachment to the approach to ethnicity adopted by the Soviet system that led to the politicization, territorialization, and hence repression of nationality could ultimately destroy Russia as well, for the same reasons it destroyed the USSR.

Those of us who want Russia to prosper, who are glad that it has reemerged from the shadow of empire, do not want to see it suffer such a fate—both from principle and out of interest. The collapse of Russia would be a real tragedy for the world and would be likely to precipitate a war far greater than we can contemplate. That is why it is so important that Russia and its leaders continue to make the shift from mission to interests, particularly in the area of their relations with the successor states. Because unless that happens, there will not be peace, stability, and progress in that part of the world, and a deterioration of those new relationships could threaten us all.

6

The U.S.-Russian Strategic Partnership

Paul D. Wolfowitz

Writing in the early part of the nineteenth century, Alexis de Tocqueville concluded the first volume of his *Democracy in America*—one of the most profound books ever written about U.S. politics—with a remarkable vision of the destinies of Russia and the United States: "Their point of departure is different and their paths diverse; nevertheless each seems called by some secret design of Providence one day to hold in its hands the destinies of half the world."

When I read this passage as a student during the cold war, it seemed prophetic, and the prophecy was a gloomy one, seeming to forecast the ideological and political conflict that would divide the United States and the Soviet Union a century and a half later: during the cold war—as in Tocqueville's time—these countries were represented by two different regimes, two different views of the individual and political life. But in that same passage, Tocqueville also saw another process under way:

> In our day, nations seem to steer toward unity. There are intellectual links between the most distant parts of the earth, and men cannot remain strangers to each other for a single day or fail to know what happens in any corner of the world. That is why one now notices less difference between contemporary Europeans and their descendants in the New World, in spite of the ocean that divides them, than there was in the thirteenth century between towns separated only by a river.

From the vantage point of the 1960s, Tocqueville's view of a world divided by two radically different societies seemed the right one. Now, in light of the emergence of a democratic Russia, as well as the rise of democratic and free market systems throughout the globe, it is perhaps Tocqueville's broader vision of nations "steering toward unity" that is truly his most prophetic insight.

National interest depends on many factors—history, geography, and economics among them—but it is not a mechanical function of those factors. Ultimately, national interest is a product of human decision. As a result, nations can make mistakes about what their national interest is—as the United States did so disastrously with its policy of isolationism between the two world wars. More fundamentally, how a nation determines its national interest will depend very much on how it is governed and by whom. The national interest of a democracy will not be the same as that of a dictatorship and will be decided differently.

Russia's historical legacy is not inevitably its destiny. One cannot ignore history, but neither should one be imprisoned by it. If nations could not escape their pasts, defense cooperation among the West European allies of the United States would not be a reality today, and democracy would not be prospering in Japan or Korea. In Russia itself we have the beginning of one of history's most dramatic examples of a nation's changing course, and it is changing Russia's view of the world as well as of itself.

Russia is now in a time of great reform, of growing democracy. What we have witnessed in 1992 and 1993 reflects a tenacious understanding of what a democratic future would mean. The long years of totalitarian rule there have not extinguished the courage and desires of the Russian people for freedom. And those people, who have suffered so greatly from communism, are now in the process of creating a better life. It is a life they deserve.

I want to state unequivocally that the United States believes in this democratic Russia. It believes in Russia's return to the world stage as a democratic nation. It does not want a hollow Russia, a Russia beset by crises. It wants a prosperous Russia, a trading partner, a democratic partner, a bulwark of security. A Russia transformed by its democratic revolution could have a healing effect on the world and bring great strength to the cause of peace. As former U.S. secretary of defense Dick Cheney has stated to the United States Congress,

> The stakes are enormous. If Russia, Ukraine, and the other states of the former Soviet Union make the transition to a new political and economic system based on Western values, then I think the next century is likely to be marked by peace and pros-

perity. If they fail, we will have to confront a new array of challenges to our security.

There are some who question whether the West truly wants to see Russia on its feet as a restored power or whether the West prefers a weak Russia. It might be thought that the Pentagon in particular would prefer a Russia that could not escape its problems. That is not the case. Let me be quite clear why.

First, even a "weak" Russia will still be strong enough to be dangerous—even fatally dangerous—and more likely to act in a dangerous way. Second, and most important, in the long run a strong Russia is most likely to come about through democratic and market reform—that is a primary lesson of the past 50 years—and these same reforms make it likely that Moscow's strength will add to the strength of our democratic allies and, therefore, be just as welcome. In so saying, the United States does not assume that its interests will always be identical with those of Russia, but most will be held in common and resolved in a manner befitting a shared democratic nature.

In truth, a strong but nondemocratic Russia would be a great problem for the United States and the West. It would certainly be a tragedy for the peoples of Russia, Eurasia, and east central Europe. The West might be forced to levels of defense spending similar to those in the cold war; it might once again face grave risks. But the hopes of the Russian people, and indeed, perhaps, of Russia's neighbors, would certainly be lost, perhaps for another 70 years. The costs of a strong, nondemocratic Russia are familiar, while the promise of a strong, democratic Russia gives added meaning to four decades of sacrifice. It would help make a better, safer world.

U.S. support lies, then, for a strong Russia, a democratic Russia, as well as for strong states throughout the former Warsaw Pact area. The United States welcomes a strong democratic Ukraine and Poland. It looks for Balts, Belorussians, Czechs, Slovaks, Hungarians, Bulgarians, and others to enrich the democratic community and add to the common security. Each has much to contribute.

Russian ambassador Vladimir Lukin has written about the role of democracy in overcoming "the total control of an all-powerful state . . . over society and the country's resources in the name of its narrow egotistical and, sometimes, expansionist aims." Democracy changes how a nation views its national interests and how it goes about securing them. A democratic Russia will find support in the community of democratic nations. Its political and economic reforms naturally link it to other democracies. No one asks Russia or any other nation to turn its back on its unique heritage. The democratic community is not a closed one. It is a community of principles—individual rights, limited and representative governments, free markets. These principles have been the basis for the peace and prosperity that unites diverse nations around the world. The United States not only welcomes Russia to its rightful place at the table; it believes Russia's success is important to its own interests.

Such a place was envisioned for Russia even at the very foundation of the West's policy of containment. Winston Churchill, in a speech better known for its warning of an "iron curtain"—a speech often cited by Soviet historians as signifying the beginning of the cold war—stated it directly:

> We welcome Russia to her rightful place among the leading nations of the world. We welcome her flag upon the seas. Above all, we welcome constant, frequent and growing contacts between the Russian people and our own people on both sides of the Atlantic.

It is only now that Russia and the West are able to fulfill the promises of cooperation that Churchill envisioned in 1946.

Shared Principles and Interests

In building its new relationship with Russia, the United States must look—as it did in the Washington Charter—toward shared principles and interests. Some conflicts of interest are inevitable, even between the closest allies. But I believe there is potentially far more to unite the two countries than to divide them, and it will be tragic if division once again prevails. It is for Russians to determine their own national interest. But how they do so will decisively shape the character of their relations with the United States and the other democracies.

A democratic Russia shares common interests and perspectives with the United States that the previous relationship obscured or even turned into causes of conflict:

1. Even at the height of the cold war, Russia and the United States had a common interest and special responsibility for the prevention of nuclear war. But the change in our political relations has transformed the character of that common interest and removed many of the old obstacles to pursuing it.

2. Russia and the United States have made more progress toward reducing nuclear weapons in the last 18 months than we achieved in 24 years of nuclear arms control negotiations. Those reductions have been truly breathtaking, eliminating whole categories of weapons that were once thought indispensable for national security.

3. Freed from the almost obsessive need to focus on the possibility of deliberate nuclear attack, the two countries have been able to reduce the alert levels of our forces safely and in ways that reduce the danger of miscalculations. Most important, we have started to discuss cooperation on ballistic missile defense, recognizing a common interest in protection against limited attacks. Although important differences remain on the subject of the Anti-Ballistic Missile (ABM) treaty, it should be possible to find common ground. We both also have an interest in halting the proliferation of weapons of mass destruction and the means for their delivery, particularly to dangerous countries like Iraq and North Korea, and in working together on a Global Protection System.

4. Both countries view the world through a wide lens. By virtue of geography and other factors, both have major interests in critical regions of the world, in particular Europe, Northeast Asia, and Southwest Asia. Under the old relationship, those interests were frequently in conflict, but with a democratic Russia many, if not all, of the conflicts disappear and significant areas of cooperation open up.

5. Russia and the United States are both Pacific nations and share a common interest in preserving stability in Northeast Asia. More and more, our policies in Korea are working in parallel to support a peaceful evolution on the peninsula and to halt North Korea's nuclear weapons efforts. The United States believes that its security relationship with Japan remains a linchpin of stability in the region, and there is no reason a democratic Russia need feel threatened by it. And both the United States and Russia have an interest in seeing the People's Republic of China (PRC) evolve along

a path that applies its growing economic strength to benefit the Chinese people and not for military purposes. And, of course, both share the risks if events in Asia go dangerously wrong.

6. For different reasons, both the United States and Russia have an interest in stability in the Persian Gulf. This common interest began to emerge after Iraq's invasion of Kuwait, when the United States achieved a level of political cooperation with the former Soviet Union that would have been inconceivable at the height of the cold war. But the United States believes that cooperation could be even stronger in the future with a democratic Russia. Indeed, as former defense secretary Cheney said to the Congress, "We could well imagine that in a crisis like Operation Desert Shield/Storm years from now, we will have not merely political, but military support from Russia, or other states of the former Soviet Union." Russian ships, for example, have already participated in the effort to enforce the UN resolutions on Iraq.

7. Given the enormous influence of Islam throughout the Persian Gulf and parts of Central Asia, both the United States and Russia have an interest in the success of moderate, democratically oriented forces as opposed to religious extremists. Fortunately, the great majority of the Muslim world wants to be a part of the modern, progressive world, and both countries should work to keep the door open to them. In this regard, the United States believes Turkey has a particularly important and positive role to play in regard to the countries of Central Asia.

A "Zone of Peace"

Of all the critical regions, none has been the source of more tragedy for Russia and the United States than Europe, the battlefield of two world wars and the birthplace of the cold war. But it is also where the cold war came to an end, and the end of the division of Europe presents us with two challenges: how to preserve the unprecedented peace and stability that Western Europe has enjoyed for the last 40 years, and how to nurture an environment in which the new democracies of central and Eastern Europe can prosper.

The first achievement is not one to take for granted. The integration of the liberal democracies, under the leadership of the United States, into a system of collective defense that has no historical precedent has been one of the major achievements of the past

40 years. For now, at least, a "zone of peace" has been achieved in North America, Western Europe, and Japan within which, it is fair to say, war is truly unthinkable. Given the history of the twentieth century, this is no mean feat—and preserving it is an objective of the first importance.

The United States will do so because it is in our national interest, but it is also in the interest of Russia and the other new democracies of Europe. One of the ironies of the end of the cold war is that the North Atlantic Treaty Organization (NATO) and the other integrating institutions of Western Europe introduce a stability that serves the interest of Russia as well.

Perhaps the greatest challenge lies in extending that democratic "zone of peace" to include the new democracies. The West wants to see that the tremendous changes in Europe further the stability, peace, and prosperity of the Continent as a whole. It does not want to find that it has torn down one wall only to erect another that divides Europe into stable and unstable halves.

Russia is forming relations with a number of new states that were formerly part of the Russian or Soviet Empire. Russia and Ukraine, perhaps the most important example, share a number of common cultural and linguistic roots but are forging separate ways in the world. The United States recognizes that many difficult and painful issues remain to be resolved between the two. As an outside observer, however, it can only admire the constructive and businesslike manner in which Presidents Boris Yeltsin and Leonid Kravchuk and their colleagues have thus far worked to resolve issues where no consensus was readily apparent. The continuation of that peaceful approach to resolving differences will have a decisive impact on Russia's relations with the West. But it will have an even more decisive effect on Russia's own hopes for prosperity and democratic progress.

There is a dramatic contrast between the ethnic violence that is tearing apart the former Yugoslavia and the ethnic peace that largely prevails between Russia and its neighbors. But there are more than enough problems to remind Americans how narrow the dividing line can be between those two situations and how difficult it is to go back once that line has been crossed.

Some nations are marked by a natural state of ethnic exclusivity, but many states, particularly in Europe today, are ethnically mixed. In such states, ethnic pride can be a source of strength and achievement, but ethnic exclusivity can prove a short step away from ethnic hatred. Ethnic hatred holds the potential for violence and tragedy or, worst of all, unspeakable crimes like the "ethnic cleansing" of today.

The United States is ethnically diverse. Americans find such diversity a source of great strength both domestically and in their dealings in a smaller and smaller world. Certainly, such diversity causes us problems, problems we are a long way from fully resolving, but we value its gifts among our greatest treasures. And because Americans know the difficult side of ethnicity, we know there are no easy answers. There are, however, some clear lessons. Governments cannot stop ethnic hatred overnight; but governments must accept the duty to control it, and governments that inflame it bear a responsibility that a generation of bold leaders may not extinguish. Once these fires are set, no one can tell where they will end or who they will burn.

For that reason, the United States shares a common interest in working to see that the human rights of all are respected. The protections of the United Nations Declaration of Human Rights and of the Helsinki Final Act and other Conference on Security and Cooperation in Europe (CSCE) and international agreements on human rights speak to all peoples. There is really no civilized alternative to ensuring the basic human rights of everyone.

A Free Market

Finally, the United States and Russia have a common interest in one another's economic prosperity. The United States wants to do its part in helping Russia make the difficult transition to a market economy. The Group of Seven, or G–7, countries meeting over the past two years have sought technical means for providing further assistance for the transformation, namely, an important $24 billion macroeconomic assistance program for Russia. Through the Freedom Support Act, the United States has authorized billions of dollars of bilateral assistance and contributions to multilateral aid institutions that will be channeled to the former Soviet states. But the main responsibility for Russia's future prosperity lies with the Russians themselves, who face a difficult process no nation has gone through before. The final curse of the Communist economy that impoverished Russia is the lack of resources or a legal framework that could ease the pain of transition to the free market system that can rejuvenate the country. There are no roadmaps, but there are some basic directions for a guide. In the end only a free market will bring prosperity, and only the forces of a free market in a proper legal framework will get Russia under way. Westerners must be careful not to preach, but it is in our interest to help as much as we can.

In the long run, one important way the West can help is to work to pursue and expand a world market in which Russia and all other countries can sell their products. Failure to do so in an earlier period was a major factor leading to the Great Depression of the 1930s, an economic catastrophe that brought with it political and military disasters as well.

The above list is by no means exhaustive. It does, however, provide a basis for reflection on practical steps Russia and the United States could take to make our partnership more concrete. A strategic partnership between the United States and Russia would continue to carry out the tasks inherited from our common efforts to dismantle the most dangerous aspects of cold war competition between the United States and the USSR. But it would go beyond those efforts to set a new agenda. Together, the West and Russia are already giving form to a new kind of relationship that looks to a democratic Russia taking its rightful place in the "zone of peace" that joins the democracies together.

Refashioning Policy

Immediately after the breaching of the Berlin Wall, the West and the United States sought to refashion their own policies to encourage and support the reforms going on in the former Soviet Union and to ease—to the extent possible—the entry of Russia and the other new states into this community of free nations. Let me mention three areas in which there have been important changes over the past few years: alliance policies that reach out to Russia, Ukraine, and the East; bold initiatives in the nuclear area; and significant changes in the U.S. defense strategy and reductions in U.S. forces.

Changes in NATO

The nations of the Atlantic Alliance have sought to reach out and welcome Russia to the community of democratic nations and to seek broad ground for cooperation. At the NATO Summit of July 1990, for example, they undertook a fundamental restructuring of NATO's strategy away from forward defense and "flexible response"—with its implications of heavy reliance on nuclear weapons—toward a new strategy enunciated by the NATO leaders to make nuclear weapons truly "weapons of last resort." That new strategy sought not only to adjust to the reduced threat but, equally, to reassure NATO's former adversaries of the truly defensive nature of the alliance.

At Copenhagen in July 1991, the NATO foreign ministers noted that the "long decades of European division are over." The Copenhagen Declaration welcomed increased contacts and committed the alliance to "seek to build constructive partnerships . . . to promote security and stability in a free and undivided Europe." Several months later, at the Rome Summit meeting of the NATO heads of state, the alliance welcomed the events that led to the rebirth of Russia and pledged to help in the effort "to build a new future based upon democracy, human rights, the rule of law, and economic liberty."

In December 1992, the alliance took an important step to reach out to the new democracies not merely as former adversaries but as future partners by creating the North Atlantic Cooperation Council (NACC). The council provides a forum to facilitate cooperation between the Western allies and the ex-Warsaw Pact countries, including the democracies of the former Soviet Union, on areas of common security concerns, including defense planning, defense conversion, and other matters relating to defense economics and budgeting.

The West is finding various ways to work with the new democracies in reshaping their defense postures. For example, through defense-to-defense contacts, NATO and the NACC can be an excellent source of information for helping to transform the offensive military doctrine of the former Warsaw Pact states into defensive doctrine. This transformation is as much about moving them away from past militarism as it is about moving societies toward democratic values and free markets; the more confident those states become about their security, the more they will do to direct scarce resources toward establishing democracy and free markets—a goal vitally important for the individual countries, for Europe as a whole, and for the United States.

Changes in Nuclear Posture

After the failed Soviet coup of August 1991, President George Bush saw an opportunity to put the U.S. relationship with Russia on a new basis and strengthen the hand of the democrats. At the president's direction, Secretary of Defense Cheney called a few people, including myself, to his office and asked us to consider the opportunities that had been created by the democratic leaders' victory in Moscow.

We believed that those leaders understood they could not afford to continue military spending at the levels that had obtained in the past and that those funds now would have to be used differently to make the economy work and permit democracy to succeed. We also believed that the new leaders did not see that the excessive Soviet nuclear arsenal—over which generations of arms controllers had haggled—had become even more of a threat to the Soviet people than to us. The United States could help to reduce the number of Soviet nuclear weapons and also the chances of them being caught up in political turbulence.

To take advantage of these opportunities, President Bush announced on September 27, 1991, a bold and historic initiative removing thousands of tactical nuclear weapons from U.S. forces. By making this gesture when the Soviet Union's bargaining power—in conventional realpolitik terms—was at a low point, the president not only made clear that the newly ascendant democratic leaders had nothing to fear from the United States; he also made it possible for Presidents Gorbachev and Yeltsin to respond quickly with a set of similar steps.

The point of the initiative was not just to lower the number of nuclear weapons on both sides. It was also to facilitate Russia's successful transition to democracy by liberating it from the debilitating weight of an excessively large force structure. More was accomplished by the two sides in 10 days than in any previous 10 years of arms control negotiations with the old Soviet regime. There could hardly be a clearer demonstration that the arms competition of the last 40 years had been driven primarily by the political conflict between the United States and the USSR and not, as we Americans were often told, the other way around.

In his State of the Union address on January 28, 1992, President Bush took further steps to limit modernization of U.S. strategic nuclear forces and to encourage a mutual reduction in the number of strategic nuclear weapons to levels substantially below those of the Strategic Arms Reduction Talks (START) Treaty. The January initiative capped or brought to a halt all U.S. strategic weapons modernization programs. The president also reiterated his appeal to the former Soviet republics to join with the United States in eliminating land-based ballistic missiles with multiple independently targetable reentry vehicle (MIRV) capacity. The initiative paved the way to the historic agreement Bush and Yeltsin reached in June 1992.

Changes in U.S. Defense Posture

In recognition of changes in the East, President Bush announced a new defense strategy for the United States, the most sweeping change in U.S. strategy since the doctrine of containment was adopted in the late 1940s. Guided by the new strategy, the United States is reducing its own forces significantly, eliminating almost a million personnel from the Pentagon's military and civilian rolls and another half million to a million from U.S. defense industries. These reductions have already cut force structure to its lowest level in terms of manpower since before the Korean War. Defense spending will decline almost 40 percent and, as a proportion of gross national product, will fall to the lowest percentage since before the attack on Pearl Harbor. Through arms control agreements with Russia and other states of the Commonwealth of Independent States (CIS) states, the United States will reduce its strategic nuclear forces to one-quarter of their 1990 level by early in the next decade. These are historic reductions, solidly based on long-term trends in the strategic environment.

Under the new defense strategy, the U.S. focus shifts from the traditional cold war threat to regional challenges. The United States will retain forces sufficient not only to respond to these challenges but also to remain engaged in critical regions and thus strive to preclude the emergence of threats there.

The United States judges that effective collective security is built on a solid foundation of American military capability and leadership. It sees U.S. leadership as enhancing collective action, not as an alternative to it and not as a euphemism for American domination. And although it will reduce its own forces significantly, it continues to believe that a strong U.S. defense capability enhances the security of all nations, and that the best way to court trouble in this new area is for the United States to cut its military capability too quickly or withdraw its forces from involvement abroad, once again tempting the ambitions of potential enemies and unsettling regional balances.

The United States premises the development of strategic cooperation with Russia on the health and vitality of its existing commitments to friends and allies. We want Russia to become a part of this larger community. We are not seeking to maintain a one-superpower world or to return to a nineteenth-century system of shifting alliances and fragile balances of power. No one will benefit if leading nations in Europe or the Pacific renationalize their defenses. The United States seeks rather to enhance the security of all through collective efforts that lie at the heart of our democratic zone of peace.

A U.S.-Russian Partnership

The Washington Charter signed in spring 1992 by Presidents Yeltsin and Bush codified the new state of relations between Russia and the United States. It stated that Russia and the United States "do not regard each other as adversaries and are developing a relationship of partnership and friendship." With the charter as a guide, we will be searching for new areas of cooperation, new ways of working together with Russia for the benefit of one another, our friends, and the world at large. Concretely, a U.S.-Russian partnership should entail the following elements:

Expanded political dialogue at all levels. Good progress has been made in this area. In some ways, the frequency and level of contacts are a carryover from the U.S.-Soviet relationship. But Russia and the United States must expand their horizons from their past concern with bilateral problems to issues of bilateral and multilateral cooperation.

Cooperation in multilateral institutions. The United States and Russia must work together cooperatively in multilateral institutions, such as the UN, the NACC, and the CSCE. Here the Washington Charter envisioned the United States and Russia cooperating with other members of those institutions in the areas of multilateral peacekeeping and efforts to prevent, manage, and resolve crises.

An expanded U.S.-Russian defense relationship. Our two countries need to expand our defense relationship beyond bilateral contacts at senior levels and create a broad and permanent interaction between our defense structures at various levels. The list of issues on which views should be exchanged is both broad and lengthy: future force structures, issues of concern regarding military plans and policies, the problem of conversion of the military-industrial base to civilian needs, budgeting, civilian control, civilian community-defense relations, environmental tasks, and a host of other issues that confront the military in a free society. We should look for ways to work and train together for participation in peacekeeping or other missions sponsored by the UN or the CSCE.

Regional cooperation. Russia and the United States should be willing to cooperate, as we have in our joint sponsorship of the Middle East Peace Conference, to help resolve regional issues. The Washington Charter pledges our two sides to work to strengthen "confidence and security in Asia and the Pacific region." Today, the first steps toward the realization of greater cooperation between the West and Russia in regional matters are already discernible. Russia has joined with the United States and others to provide naval forces for the Multilateral Intercept Force in the Gulf region to enforce UN sanctions against Iraq. Russian peacekeeping troops have been working in Croatia as part of the larger UN effort in the former Yugoslavia. The United States welcomes these steps and believes they augur well for broader and deeper collaborative efforts in the future. Robust Russian support for efforts strengthening peacekeeping, countering proliferation, or quelling aggression would be significant militarily as well as politically.

Cooperation on nonproliferation. As the United States and Russia move beyond dealing with the proliferation concerns raised by the collapse of the Soviet Union, we should continue to work together for the continued viability of the nuclear Non-Proliferation Treaty, the Biological Weapons Convention (BWC), the Chemical

Weapons Convention (CWC), and the Missile Technology Control Regime (MTCR).

Cooperation on measures to counter terrorism and narcotics. The U.S. and Russian militaries could explore ways to support the Washington Charter's pledge for joint cooperation on these important issues.

Yet, even as the United States develops cooperative approaches with Russia to securing our common interest, a number of concerns continue to hold the potential to disrupt progress. The failure of the new links and relationships between two countries is not inevitable, but nor is the success of our mutual efforts a certainty. One problem of particular importance is the need for thoroughgoing military reform. Russia must create a system of democratic controls on the military that will ensure public, parliamentary, and executive authority over its budget and policies. Such a system, like that established in the United States, is good not only for the people but, as U.S. military leaders will attest, for the military as well. It has provided strong material and moral support to all military services and has subjected basic U.S. strategy, policies, and programs to public and parliamentary scrutiny.

Such a system would make it impossible for Russia to continue to invest millions of rubles in military projects that make no sense in today's international environment. A case in point is the continuing, wasteful construction of deep-underground bunkers to protect leaders and military commanders from a nuclear war; these facilities serve no useful purpose in this new era. Such vestiges of an earlier era of confrontation should be swept aside by a democratic Russia. They detract from the achievement of its national interests and its mutual agenda with the United States.

If the challenges of the next decade are to be met, it is clear that Russia must be positively engaged in the world. The West needs a democratic Russia and Eurasia, serving as a bridge between the great civilizations of the world. It needs Russian reform to succeed. It wants the global trend toward democratic reforms and free markets to continue to spread throughout Eurasia. The most ambitious plans for prosperity and cooperation, whether for greater integration in Europe or an era of stability in Asia, cannot come to pass if the Eurasian land mass is an area of crisis and instability. The West wants to see a democratic, rejuvenated Russia take its rightful place on the world stage and add its voice and its power to the existing community of nations that seek peace and, when necessary, oppose aggression.

The curious cold war that has so intertwined the destinies of the United States and Russia has had a curious ending. Some of the credit for the end of the cold war must go to Western democracies, which for 40 years successfully resisted the efforts of the Soviet Union to expand by force. That success, in turn, owes a great deal to the leadership of the United States, which created the conditions necessary for the democratic nations of Europe and Asia to prosper and to provide for their common defense in a collective fashion rather than fruitlessly—and dangerously—trying to manage crises as separate nations striking out on their own. The United States worked with its allies in Europe and Asia not only to counter the Communist threat, but also to build them into countries that share basic American commitments to democracy and free markets. U.S. leaders have set before their nation as one of its principal tasks maintaining these ties and extending them to other nations that share our basic values. The United States welcomes all the states of central and Eastern Europe and Russia, Ukraine, and the other former Soviet republics into the democratic community of nations. For should the hope of this new era dim and new security challenges emerge, the United States will meet those challenges as it has in the past through the strength of collective security.

In the end, the greatest credit for the victory in the cold war must go to the peoples of the former Soviet Union and Eastern Europe and to their new democratic governments. They have demonstrated that the human spirit is stronger than even the most despotic tyranny. Although the challenges they face today are not behind them, as they turn to the difficult tasks of building societies based on law and competitive markets and, of particular interest here, of determining their national interest in this new era, they do so as free peoples and as friends of the United States.

7
Military Interests and the Interests of the Military

Sergei Rogov

The collapse of the Soviet Union has produced drastic changes in the global balance of power, which had been dominated by the United States and the USSR. The Soviet Union was for many decades able to maintain strategic parity with the United States—an equilibrium in which offensive nuclear weapons played the preponderant role. Now, a new Russian state has emerged that is politically, economically, and even geographically different from its predecessor (as well as from any Russia that existed before 1917).

Russia is undergoing a major reevaluation of its military policies, but it is already clear that in the post–cold war international system it will be at best a major player, not a superpower. In purely military terms, the collapse of the USSR meant the loss of major strategic assets. Russia's territory was substantially diminished and its resource base drastically reduced. (It has no more than 60 percent of the gross national product and population of the former Soviet Union.) Its western borders were pushed far to the east; important ports on the Baltic, Caspian, and Black Seas became "foreign." Russia's inventory of conventional weapons in Europe will be only a fraction of what the Soviet armed forces possessed, and although Soviet strategic forces were supposed to remain under the united control of the new Commonwealth of Independent States (CIS), Ukraine and other former republics are trying to claim a share of them. Finally, an entirely new structure of international relations (and with it, new security problems for Russia) has been created by the emergence of independent states in Central Asia and the Transcaucasus.

The fact that it cannot be a superpower does not mean that Russia should disarm, but there is no need to continue an arms race that was too great a burden even for the 15 republics of the former USSR. Far from competing with former Soviet republics and major powers like the United States, Western Europe, the People's Republic of China (PRC), and Japan, Russia needs reliable partners and allies. Our nation has a vital interest in reorienting its efforts to assure a better life for its population and to deal with the real threats to its security, which now arise largely from internal, not external, sources. This is why the national interests of Russia in the military field can be defined mainly in negative terms: to prevent foreign states from threatening Russia's territorial integrity, the economic and social well-being and human rights of its citizens, or its democratic political system.

This redefinition of military interests is reflected in the debate over Russia's new defense doctrine, according to which it regards no specific state, or coalition of states, as an enemy. Instead, its military experts distinguish between "threats" and "risks." Risks include such problems as the following: the large peacetime armies and high mobilization potential retained by some states; national, ethnic, religious, and ideological conflicts that are still a source of war and conflict; the hegemonic ambitions of some states, whether globally or regionally; and potential changes of leadership or political and economic crises in other states that could lead to basic changes in their attitude toward the outside world.

These risks are a reminder that military power remains an important factor of national security and that Russia may encounter a resurgence of foreign threats in the future.

Military Interests in the Former Soviet Republics

The first priority of Russian security policy should be to establish good relations with its closest circle of states, other former Soviet republics. Territorial and ethnic conflicts with these republics pose the greatest external threat to Russia; conflicts in Moldova, Abkhazia, South Ossetia, Nagorno-Karabakh, and Tajikistan have already threatened to spill across Russia's borders.

Given this vulnerability, conservatives in the military complain about the very strict limits imposed on Russia's armed forces by the November 1990 Conventional Forces in Europe (CFE) treaty and about national ceilings for CIS states agreed to in Tashkent in May 1992. Some of these complaints make sense. (It is, for example, difficult to accept the idea that the northern flank of Russia—with a border more than 1,000 miles long—can be adequately defended by one active motorized rifle brigade and one or two additional brigades with their equipment pre-positioned in POMCUS-type storage!)

Yet no one should think Russia's geography allows it to build a new "Maginot Line" around its borders. It is simply impossible to restore the Soviet posture of "forward defenses." Instead, Russia needs a friendly environment that will preclude confrontation of any kind with its closest neighbors.

The newly independent states, moreover, hardly represent a traditional military threat to Russia. It is very difficult to imagine a situation in which one of the former Soviet republics would actually "invade" Russia. For this reason, the armed forces of Russia should not build up large concentrations of troops on the borders with Ukraine, Belarus, and Kazakhstan. To protect its western and southern borders, Russia has no need for Soviet-style ground forces, with more than a hundred heavy tank and motorized rifle divisions. At the same time, the high risk of local or border conflicts means that it does need specially trained light forces, which (as the war in Afghanistan showed) can be much more effective than heavy divisions.

Ideally, Russia and the former Soviet republics would agree on common defense arrangements that would extend the air defense zone of Russia and thereby exclude any danger of a land attack from either the west or the south. Russia would in this way be able to preserve the early warning system of the USSR, which will help to enhance strategic stability.

Such cooperation could evolve into an integrated common defense organization on the model of the North Atlantic Treaty Organization (NATO). If so, the Supreme Command of the Unified Armed Forces of the CIS would become a truly joint structure, with permanent participation by representatives of the member states and rotation of major positions in the command and joint staff offices.

Short of this, Russia should try to reach bilateral agreements, especially with Ukraine and Belarus, that allow it to use certain military facilities on their territory. With its tremendous defense industry, Russia may be able to preserve its position as the only military supplier to those states. At a minimum, Russia would also probably try to preclude the participation of the new states in any hostile military alliances or the stationing of foreign troops (or use of military facilities) by other states on the territory of the former Soviet republics.

Discussion of such defense relationships among the members of the CIS will be an open-ended process that can evolve in different directions. It can lead to a true military and political alliance, or instead to a "civilized divorce"—a peaceful division of the former Soviet military assets.

Unfortunately, the military dispute between Russia and Ukraine threatens both of those outcomes. Although much attention has centered on the issue of the Black Sea fleet, the most acute problem involves strategic nuclear forces deployed in Ukraine. It is becoming clearer all the time that Ukraine wants to become a nuclear power. It sees in nuclear weapons a kind of insurance against possible Russian meddling in its domestic affairs—even against the risk that Ukraine, which has never existed as an independent state within its present borders, might disintegrate. Kazakhstan may have similar views, and if these two hold on to erstwhile Soviet weapons, Belarus may well follow suit. If the former Soviet nuclear arsenal is divided in this fashion, many other states around the world will also review their nuclear aspirations, and the entire nuclear nonproliferation regime could collapse.

Ukrainian policy to date has been successful in protecting a nuclear option in part because of a lack of clarity in U.S. policy. The Lisbon Protocol signed in May 1992 recognized Russia, Ukraine, Kazakhstan, and Belarus as equal "successors" in implementing the Strategic Arms Reduction Talks (START I) Treaty. Ukraine in this way became a party to decisions about how to distribute "ceilings and limitations" established by the treaty and gained control over reductions taking place on its territory.

The United States considered the Lisbon Protocol a success because of article 5, in which Ukraine, Kazakhstan, and Belarus promised to join the nuclear Non-Proliferation Treaty (NPT) as nonnuclear powers. But this was hardly an achievement. Ukraine and Belarus are already constitutionally pledged to join the NPT, and they made a binding international commitment to this effect in the Alma-Ata agreement in December 1991. Moreover, article 5 of the Lisbon Protocol contains no timetable.

In general, Ukrainian policy makes a joke of the whole idea of nonnuclear status by refusing to recognize Russia as the owner of the nuclear weapons on Ukrainian territory. (In fact, just the opposite occurred in July 1993, when Ukraine declared "ownership" of the weapons.) It now seems likely that national security considerations will be the pretext for an eventual Ukrainian refusal to denuclearize.

Ukraine is also trying to impose unreasonable demands on Russia, which it knows will never be accepted, to avoid having to give up its nuclear forces. Russia, for example, can hardly agree, as Ukraine is demanding, to the idea of "international control" over the dismantling of weapons under START as proposed in June 1993 by the United States; this would be a unilateral change in the terms of the treaty. Finally, President Leonid Kravchuk's demand that the weapons be destroyed in Ukraine amounts to a demand that new facilities be built in his country for the dismantling—but equally, of course, for the assembly—of nuclear weapons.

The commitments that Ukraine has made to date can, in other words, eventually serve as a justification for it to become a full-fledged nuclear power. Russian policy itself sometimes seems to help this along. For instance, under pressure from the General Staff, Russia seems willing to postpone totally removing the multiple warhead capacity of intercontinental ballistic missiles (ICBMs) until 2005 and to allow at least some nuclear weapons to remain in Kazakhstan even after the seven-year period of the implementation of the START I treaty.

Nuclear issues are the most explosive element of Russia's relations with former Soviet states. Time is not on Russia's side, however, but on that of Ukraine and Kazakhstan, which have a clear interest in delay. Russia's interests, by contrast, require an early resolution of these problems. Without it, political dynamics within the Commonwealth may bring Russia to a point of no return.

Military Interests in Eurasia

Beyond the "near abroad," Russia has important security interests in a second circle of states—in central and Eastern Europe, the Middle East, and the Far East. This second circle includes at least three of the major centers of power in the multipolar post–cold war world. It also brings Russia into contact with the heart of the Islamic world. Even Russia's control over its own territory in Siberia and the Far East can be jeopardized by conflicts with China or Japan, both of which have territorial claims against the Russian Federation.

Today there is no military threat to Russia from this second circle of states, but a number of threats may emerge in the future. Although Sino-Russian relations are now very good, China clearly remains a source of potential military danger. A large-scale military conflict with the PRC would be a nightmare for Russia. Russia's population is only one-eighth that of China; the Chinese are also surpassing Russia economically and will draw even technologically in the next century.

This is not the only threat that Russia may face. Turkey, Iran, Afghanistan, Pakistan, and some other Middle Eastern states are becoming more involved in violent conflicts in Central Asia and the Transcaucasus, where Russia's security interests are obvious.

In anticipating these and other threats, Russia can no longer be sure of either qualitative or quantitative advantages in the event of conflict. The implementation of the CFE treaty is transforming the European military landscape. Whereas the Soviet Union once dominated, NATO has now become the overwhelming military force in Europe, with three times as many ground weapons and twice as many airplanes and helicopters as Russia. This may explain why the NATO countries did not openly object when Ukraine and other former Soviet republics sought large shares of the Soviet CFE quota. Manpower and equipment levels for Ukraine and Belarus are extremely high in relation to other European powers, but for the West the result was a drastic cut in Russian military potential.

The military balance created by the CFE treaty means that for the foreseeable future Russia will not be able to act alone. Russia will have an interest in multilateral arrangements both within the evolving European security system and within the CIS.

Political instability in the East European states, difficult economic problems, violent ethnic conflicts, lack of strict political control over military and paramilitary forces, and huge inventories of weaponry—all these trends may have serious consequences for peace and stability in Europe. Already there are or have been four shooting wars in Europe—in the former Yugoslavia, Moldova, and Georgia, and between Armenia and Azerbaijan.

What are the military implications of this new environment? First of all, Russia will need a strategic reserve of highly mobile conventional forces, concentrated near the Urals, that would allow it to project power from within its territory. This approach may also include pre-positioning of some heavy weapons and equipment in the three major military theaters, but without permanent stationing of large and fully mobilized forces there.

A second implication involves the role of tactical nuclear weapons. Given a NATO residual force of tactical nuclear weapons, plus the Chinese factor, it is difficult for Russia to give up its tactical nuclear weapons unilaterally. Some military experts have actually suggested that Russia *upgrade* the role of nuclear weapons in its defense doctrine, using them to deter any war against itself. Others have proposed that Russia withdraw Leonid Brezhnev's no-first-use pledge, a step affirmed by the new military doctrine decreed by Boris Yeltsin in November 1993.

The legacy of the cold war has not been fully overcome. Even after all CFE reductions are made, there will still be many more tanks in Europe than there were in 1945. These high levels of armament, together with growing instability in some regions, increase the risk of a revival of military confrontation. That is why the CFE treaty should be seen not as an end point but as a first step in a radical transformation of military postures and establishments "from Vancouver to Vladivostok." This will also allow fulfillment of the legitimate security interests of Russia. For while Russia cannot be a superpower, it will be one of the most important participants in any efforts to maintain international peace and stability.

Military Interaction between Russia and the United States

Relations with "the West," especially the United States, form the third circle of Russia's security interests. Russian participation in European and North Atlantic integration may also play a decisive role in the future of democratic institutions and a market economy in Russia itself. If Russia is not involved in this integration, its economic progress will be in doubt and its "Eurasian" character might become more Asian.

Even after radical cuts in the strategic nuclear forces of both sides (down to 75 to 80 percent of present levels), Russia will remain the only power able to threaten the national existence of the United States. At a minimum, this means that nuclear issues left over from the previous historical period will continue to need very delicate joint management. Beyond this, however, a more fundamental transformation of the military relationship between the two sides is now possible and desirable. Russian efforts should be directed at creating a mutual security regime with the United States, a kind of limited partnership based on the fact that the two countries' interests now converge on all of the most important military issues facing them. This is true whether the issue is strengthening strategic stability, preventing the proliferation of nuclear, biological, and chemical weapons, or discouraging Japan and Germany from translating their economic power into military capability.

This new level of understanding goes far beyond détente, just as it goes beyond the cold war. The cooperation that is now possible between Russia and the United States is, in fact, like the cooperation of allies. The aim, however, should not be to create a traditional military alliance, which requires a common enemy, but to tackle common problems.

A Russian-American mutual security regime would extend to almost all aspects of military policy and practice. It would involve, among other actions, the disengagement of military forces in those regions where they directly oppose each other and where there is extreme danger of the immediate emergence of military conflict; limitation of some types of military activities, including the scale and zones of maneuvers; steps to increase transparency; and quantitative and qualitative limits on the arms race.

In a subsequent stage, joint decision making might take up such questions as limitations on military research and development, reduction of defense budgets, and implementation of constructive military conversion. True mutual security would require a truly common threat assessment; it would make possible a coordination of Russian and American plans for new armaments—which new weapons could be deployed and which could not. In this way, interaction in the military sphere would become genuinely nonthreatening and acquire a cooperative and nonconfrontational basis.

Some of these cooperative activities may emerge only in the distant future. For now, let us discuss the kind of cooperation that is clearly foreseeable within this decade.

Joint management of the nuclear legacy. It is hard to break out of the relationship of mutual deterrence that was created in the cold war, but it is necessary. Even if both parties have no hostile intentions, the existence of residual strategic forces could lead to a revival of political tensions between the United States and Russia. Russia's goal, then, is to strengthen deterrence in the short term while trying at the same time to move beyond it to a relationship based on different principles.

The START II agreement reached by Presidents Bush and Yeltsin in June 1992 and January 1993 strengthens deterrence through a fundamental restructuring of strategic forces. The new nuclear postures of Russia and the United States will effectively rule out many of the escalation scenarios that preoccupied both sides during the cold war. Deterrence remains, but it is truly aimed at preventing nuclear war rather than at controlling escalation.

This breakthrough should be the starting point for further steps toward a new strategic interrelationship. These steps might include such measures as creation of permanent mechanisms for consultation and oversight of the activities of both strategic forces, with permanent liaison offices between the Russian General Staff and the American Joint Chiefs of Staff; enhanced cooperation in the area of early warning, including joint launch and operation of satellites; limits on potentially provocative military activities, including sanctuaries for submarines; cooperation in the safe maintenance, transfer, storage, and dismantlement of nuclear warheads; and, finally, development of a joint approach to nuclear testing.

Perhaps the most important near-term measure to deal with the nuclear legacy would be to remove from alert status all (or almost all) Russian and U.S. strategic nuclear forces. Certainly, all weapons to be reduced under START I and START II could be taken off alert immediately. Similarly, all weapons could be removed from heavy bombers and stored away from bomber bases. Submarine patrols could be cut back, and submarines in port taken off alert. Only a small number of ICBMs (perhaps 100) should remain on alert.

Such arrangements would eventually allow Russia and the United States to move beyond deterrence for good. The capacity for mutual destruction should not lock us into confrontation. The example of Great Britain and France proves that nuclear powers have options other than deterrence.

Control over transfer of weapons and military technology. As Russia and the United States reduce their own military capabilities, neither country wants others to replace them as "superpowers" or to achieve an equal level of military power. We have a major security interest, then, in managing the emerging multipolar balance of forces.

Of first importance is the goal of preventing the collapse of the nuclear nonproliferation regime. Nuclear weapons can be "the great equalizer." An increase in the size of the nuclear club would complicate Russian and American efforts to reduce nuclear forces and improve strategic stability. For this reason, keeping nuclear weapons out of the hands of other former Soviet states is an immediate priority. The United States, Russia, and Great Britain—as the depositories of the NPT—should issue an invitation to the successor states to sign the NPT by a certain date. If they decline, some means of political and economic pressure should be considered.

If Russia and the United States can agree on verification measures for the dismantling of nuclear weapons and the disposition of the resulting plutonium, they may be able to push for a much stronger plutonium regime under the International Atomic Energy Agency. Stronger control is needed for the entire plutonium cycle; violators of this regime should face reprisals from the international community.

Cooperation between Russia and the United States is also necessary to close loopholes in controls over other weapons of mass destruction, which are getting cheaper and easier to acquire. The United States should consider helping Russia to overcome financial and technological obstacles in implementing the Soviet-American chemical weapons agreement; without help, the elimination of chemical weapons may be delayed.

As for the proliferation of ballistic missiles, Russia is still not a full participant in the ballistic missile control regime. One result was the 1993 dispute about the missile technology sale to India.

Russia must formally join this control regime, which itself needs strengthening, particularly to make it more difficult to extend the range and capabilities of short-range surface-to-surface and surface-to-air missiles.

The end of the cold war has increased the pressure on the world's arms manufacturers to find new buyers, especially in the developing world. Coordination between Russia and the United States is necessary here; some sort of market sharing may have to be considered to prevent the transfer of sophisticated, dangerous military technologies. It is not in either side's interest to promote the buildup of China, India, and some countries in the Middle East.

Cooperation in international peacekeeping. Outside of the three "circles" that have been described, Russia has no vital security interests globally. But even if events in South America or Africa have no direct impact on it, the Russian Federation, as one of the great powers, should fulfill its responsibilities for international peacekeeping—and even peacemaking—under the United Nations (UN) umbrella. It may now be possible for the UN to perform those functions that were envisioned in its charter but never realized because of the cold war.

The UN Military Staff Committee must be revitalized if the UN is to perform its peacekeeping role. To be effective, the committee needs a small permanent force, most of whose troops would come from neutral or nonaligned nations; permanent use of units of the great powers' armed forces should be avoided. In addition, the committee should build a system of staff, communication, and logistical support, including air-lift and sea-lift capabilities for UN forces. Finally, in emergency cases, certain designated units of the great powers, among them permanent members of the Security Council, should be available for use with Security Council authorization.

Although the Russian and U.S. operational role should be limited, it should be clear that multinational forces can rely on the full power of permanent members of the Security Council and that, when needed, the 18th Airborne Corps and Marines of the United States, or some Russian air-mobile forces, can be quickly engaged to stop aggression and enforce peace. A small multinational naval force under the UN flag might also be considered to protect freedom of navigation; American and Russian involvement in such a force could be more substantial than in operations on land.

Naturally, representatives of the designated great-power forces must conduct joint staff exercises and maintain other permanent links. Interaction between Russia and the United States under such multilateral auspices could be even easier to establish than in a bilateral framework.

Major Interests of the Military

The collapse of the USSR subjected the members of the Soviet military to tremendous pressure. They found themselves an army without a state. To probe their attitudes, in February 1992 the Armed Forces Center for Sociological, Psychological, and Legal Studies conducted a poll among 1,200 officers and warrant officers at 10 military bases in the Russian Federation. The poll found an unprecedented level of unhappiness, a growing polarization of opinions, and a deepening mistrust of political authorities. Although 90 percent believed that the military should stay out of politics, only 17 percent supported the policies of the Russian government. Eighty-four percent believed social tensions were likely to keep growing, perhaps resulting in public riots.

According to another poll taken at about the same time, 67 percent of officers opposed the breakup of the armed forces of the Soviet Union. In yet another survey, this one of the participants in the Officers' Assembly on January 17, 1992 (the first effort in many decades to organize the military into a separate political force), 78 percent of senior officers and 55 percent of junior officers supported the restoration of the Soviet Union.

This situation of military estrangement from the state began to change only after Russia decided to create its own armed forces, into which most former Soviet military personnel were absorbed. On May 7, 1992, President Yeltsin signed the decree "On Creation of the Armed Forces of the Russian Federation," and since then the Russian defense minister, General Pavel Grachev, has issued plans for reorganizing the armed forces in three stages between now and the end of the century.

This gradual approach, although reflecting the desires of the military establishment to slow down force reductions and postpone long-overdue reforms, greatly complicates the problems facing the Russian military. Yet it is a natural and predictable result of the current fluidity of Russian politics. Like other special interest groups in post-Soviet society, the military feel free to put forward their demands and present their own special interests as national interests. In contrast to the strict control the Communist Party exerted over the Soviet armed forces, today's military is almost totally on its own and has begun more and more actively to push its own demands forward.

In the next several years, keeping the former Soviet military under civilian political control, while simultaneously reducing its size and dividing it into several allied armies, will be an immense task. To date, no civilian institution has shown that it can exert such control.

Military interests can be divided into four major groups of concerns: social conditions, career opportunities, technical equipment, and internal divisions in the armed forces.

Social conditions. According to official figures, about 105,000 officers and warrant officers in Russia lack housing. The problem is aggravated by the redeployment of forces from Germany, Poland, the Baltic states, and other former Soviet republics. Before long, the number of homeless officers may reach 300,000.

Low pay is another serious problem. A generation ago the income of military officers was twice as high as the income of civilians with comparable educational and professional levels; now it is the same or lower. Families that depend on two salaries to get by find relocation especially difficult because it is very hard for military wives to find new employment.

Official policy currently does very little to solve these social problems. The Ministry of Defense constructed 35,000 apartments in 1991 and 41,000 in 1992, but these are not nearly enough to meet the needs of the present officer corps. Meanwhile, most of the money allocated for military construction, which in 1992 exceeded 11 percent of the defense budget, goes not into housing but into construction of new bases and facilities for the troops that are redeployed from abroad into Russia. These numbers make it clear that the massive redeployment of forces from abroad into Russia could result in a serious social explosion with unpredictable political consequences.

Career opportunities. Career planning has become all but impossible for Russian officers. Cuts between now and 1995 will reduce the size of the armed forces, first from 2.8 million to 2.1 million, and then to 1.5 million by the year 1995. General Grachev has announced that the draft will continue, but the number of conscripts in Russia is falling. In 1989, 47 percent of draftees were exempted from service; in 1991, more than 70 percent. In 1989 there were 3,000 draft dodgers; in 1991, 17,000. Only 28 percent of all eligible young men were expected to be drafted into the armed forces in 1992. The Russian army manpower level is at least 30 percent lower than required. As a result, officers in many units have to perform the duties of enlisted men. Finding this unacceptable, more and more are looking to opportunities in the private sector.

Efforts to block military reform will not succeed. Russia does not need and cannot maintain present force levels, and the final size of the force may be as low as 1.2 million. In future it should, for military and other reasons, be an all-volunteer force. The huge exodus of officers that lies ahead demands a massive program for social rehabilitation of these people, including retraining for civilian jobs, credit, and tax benefits. Without some early government attention to this issue, the problem seems certain to be aggravated.

Technical equipment. The most modern Soviet weapons were deployed outside Russia in Eastern Europe and the western Soviet republics. As a result, Russian officers today complain about the low quality of their equipment; almost 75 percent of all Russian weapons are, they claim, obsolete. Most of them will, in fact, soon be useless, because the defense ministry lacks the means to service this huge arsenal of outdated weapons. (One example: 80 percent of all the former Soviet army's tank repair facilities were located outside Russia.)

At the same time, First Deputy Defense Minister Andrei Kokoshin has announced that defense production has been reduced by 50 to 60 percent; in some categories, output is down by 90 percent. He has also complained that Russia produces too many types of weapons: Russian forces have 63 types of armored vehicles (the U.S. Army, only 16), 62 types of guns and tactical missiles (the U.S. Army, 37), and 26 types of surface-to-air missiles (the U.S. Army, 4). Kokoshin has suggested that Russian industry should continue to manufacture only one of four types of weapons. If this approach is accepted, the result will be an extremely long process of rearmament. The quality of arms may eventually be rather high, but during the transition period the combat readiness of the Russian armed forces will be seriously diminished.

Internal divisions. Dividing the Soviet armed forces has turned out to be extremely difficult in human terms. Many Russian officers now find themselves serving in foreign armies. In fact, the officer corps in Ukraine, Belarus, and Kazakhstan is mostly Russian; only 4 percent of the officers of the armed forces of Belarus can speak Belorussian. Although most military personnel have accepted this political change, some officers in areas of conflict like Moldova or the Transcaucasus have sold weapons to the warring parties or become mercenaries—a reflection of the demoralization that afflicts the post-Soviet military institution in general.

There are also many officers of non-Russian origin still serving in the Russian armed forces. Of several hundred thousand officers and warrant officers of Ukrainian origin, only 10,000 have asked to be transferred to Ukraine. The rest want to continue to serve in the Russian army.

Political divisions within society divide the officers as well. Left-wing and right-wing organizations of officers are now actively engaged in political activities. More generally, the widespread confusion of the Russian government encourages the military establishment to become more active in efforts to protect its interests. Lacking political guidance from the government, officers have initiated their own debates about military doctrine and present force structure.

The transformation of the former Soviet military machine creates major challenges for Russia and other new states that emerged from the collapse of the Soviet Union. Creating its own forces will hardly be easy for Russia. But the success of the process will be of crucial importance for efforts in many other areas—for the parallel efforts of other former Soviet republics, for the creation of a common defense system for the Commonwealth of Independent States, and for the defense of Russian interests both in the "near abroad" and beyond.

8
Adapting to the World Economy: Interests and Obstacles

Anders Åslund

Discussion on the place and concept of Russia in the world has only just begun. Although Russia has many opportunities open to it, they may not be as numerous as is widely expected. The purpose of this essay is, first, to examine the restrictions of the old command economy and, second, to contrast them with the new preconditions of a market economy. Third, I shall assess the consequences of this economic revolution for Russia's foreign trade. Next, I shall consider what the Russian government could do in the new setting in relation to the former Soviet republics and to the outside world. Finally, I shall discuss what the plausible consequences of the preferred choices would be and which issues remain open. Eventually, we must pose the question: What is the appropriate concept of Russia's place in the world?

Former Restrictions in Foreign Economic Relations

The Communist economic system was full of restrictions.[1] The most essential constraint was that foreign trade was supposed to be both politically controlled and politically oriented before economic issues were addressed. One of the most obvious political consequences was that foreign trade was concentrated on socialist countries. For instance, in 1987, 67 percent of Soviet foreign trade was with socialist countries, although this trade accounted for only 4 percent of world trade. Another major political aim of Soviet foreign trade was to gain the sympathies of developing countries, in part through large transfers of resources. Similarly, the USSR subsidized huge exports of arms. Of its total arms exports from 1985 until 1990, only 33 percent were paid for directly; credits were issued for 40 percent, mostly on very favorable conditions, and 27 percent were free or heavily subsidized.[2] The total political costs of

83

the old foreign trade policy were huge, although it is not easy to assess which costs and distortions pertain to sheer politics and which are inherent in the socialist economic system.

Apart from the political constraints, the nature of the command economy imposed yet others. First, the state monopoly of foreign trade was a fundamental aspect of Communist economics. The state was expected to control trade in each commodity through one central body, and the result was enormous centralization. Second, central planning demanded a high degree of stability: influences from foreign trade were not allowed to disturb the domestic economy, although imports were utilized to fill holes in the domestic supply system. Third, a non-market economy required far-reaching protectionism because any kind of "freer trade" would imply competition and thus market-economy tendencies that could not be tolerated—from neither an ideological nor a bureaucratic point of view. The bureaucrats' disdain for competition was compatible with, and supported by, the ideological demands of Communism. Fourth, as a consequence of all these economic restrictions, domestic prices of imports as well as exports were set arbitrarily with little regard for world market prices, production costs, or scarcity. Domestic prices had no relation to foreign trade prices. The differences between these prices varied greatly, amounting to hefty foreign trade taxes or subsidies.

In the end, the foreign trade system that had developed was riddled with idiosyncrasies. Although it was a reasonably consistent system, in which political and economic principles reinforced one another, nothing in the system rewarded economic rationality or efficiency. Therefore, the longer the socialist foreign trade system existed, the more irrational and inefficient it became, despite substantial market-oriented aberrations in the pricing. The system that had put such a premium on stability was undermined because of its inability to generate the only source of stability that counts in the long run: economic dynamism.

New Conditions for Foreign Trade Created by a Market Economy

The ideas of a market economy are extremely distant from those of a command economy in the sphere of foreign trade. While the

command economy is based on the rights of the state, the market
economy is based on the rights of the individual economic enterprise. These enterprises must have the right to engage freely in foreign trade with few restrictions. They may choose to do so at a
loss, but their basic motive in foreign trade is to achieve profits. It is
this conceptual change that must take place in Russia.

A number of consequences follow from this simple statement:

- First, no monopoly of foreign trade is acceptable in a market economy, neither one controlled by the state nor one
  controlled by anyone else, because that would limit freedom of enterprise.

- Second, with or without trade restrictions, prices in foreign
  trade must be set in free negotiations between the firms involved, because no one should be allowed to dictate commercial conditions to an independent firm. In principle,
  subsidies are not acceptable, while low customs tariffs are
  the rule.

In a market economy, however, the state also has an interest in
foreign trade. A major task in the building of a market economy is
the development of sufficient competition so that domestic markets become reasonably balanced. The liberalization of foreign
trade is one useful means of boosting domestic competition. Another interest of the state is to balance foreign trade, which also implies a stabilization of the domestic economy. The state therefore
needs to liberalize foreign trade and to establish a competitive exchange rate so that exports can balance imports.

One part of this scenario is the liberalization of the currency.
There is little point in introducing a unified customs tariff without
unifying the exchange rate, and the exchange rate needs to be stabilized. This can be accomplished in several ways, but the underly-
ing conditions should be a relatively free foreign trade and an exchange rate that corresponds to the country's ability to earn foreign
currency revenues.

Naturally, there is little room for political interference in the
new market economy. Because of the liberalization of prices, the
actual costs of all state intervention can easily be assessed, and
they are not likely to appear tolerable.

Consequences of the Transition to Free Foreign Trade

As one can easily guess from this quick look at the basic principles of the old and new foreign trade systems in Russia, massive changes can be expected in the actual performance of foreign trade. An initial conclusion is that there is no longer room for the Council for Mutual Economic Assistance (CMEA or COMECON), with its bilateral barter in five-year packages and artificial allocation of production. The CMEA's very principles were inspired by central planning. Moreover, its pricing mechanism led to overpricing of manufactured goods and underpricing of raw materials. When most of the CMEA countries had switched to market economies, the demise of the CMEA trading system was inevitable. The consequence was an extraordinary disruption of trade: the trade volume among the formerly socialist countries collapsed by about two-thirds in 1990/1991. There was little complementarity between the formerly socialist countries because economic rationality had been disregarded in the development of this trade.

Another consequence was a swift change in terms of trade that benefited the producers of raw materials, essentially the USSR. Both the Soviet Union and Eastern Europe, however, found that they had no buyers for their superfluous goods within their old trading community. The East Europeans could not afford to buy Soviet raw materials in nearly as large quantities after prices were liberalized and reached world market levels. The USSR, on the other hand, found the prices demanded by the East Europeans for their substandard manufactured goods excessive. In addition, the goods suffered from a bad reputation. Moreover, there was no functioning payments system, and there was a shortage of both liquidity and trust. The collapse of intra-CMEA trade appeared inevitable. In 1991, trade within the region of Eastern Europe and the USSR accounted for only 25 percent of all foreign trade in the region.[3] The collapse continued through 1992. Soon countries like Poland will carry out only about one-tenth of their trade with former CMEA countries.

In 1992, a similar collapse of trade started among the former states of the USSR. There is no indication that the collapse there will be any less dramatic. On the contrary, there are many reasons why it may go further than in Eastern Europe. The economic distortions are much more developed in the former USSR because of a longer period of Communism and a more ruthless non-economic rule. Transportation costs on land will doubtless become enormous when ordinary market-oriented transport tariffs are introduced. An extraordinary disorder prevails in the former USSR, and economic decline has been greater the more backward and disorganized an economy has been. The distrust of neighbors is generally greater in countries that have just split from one another. In 1992–1993, interstate trade in the former USSR has declined no less than two-thirds.

Meanwhile, East European trade is swiftly being reoriented toward the West, although it might suffer confusion arising from two factors. On the one hand, trade is being redirected toward the dominant trading nations, which are Western. On the other hand, in line with the gravity theory, trade is geared toward neighboring countries, which are West European. In the case of Russia, however, it would be natural if trade were boosted also with East Asia, including Japan, the People's Republic of China (PRC), and South Korea, and with the United States, which is relatively near. During the first year of systemic change, East European countries expanded their exports to the West by 25 to 45 percent. Russia did far worse in 1992 because of a much more gradual liberalization and little stabilization of the Russian economy, but this merely signifies that the expansion of trade with the West is delayed. Russia has more readily exportable goods than any country in Eastern Europe. With sufficient liberalization of its foreign trade, combined with a macroeconomic stabilization, Russia's raw materials and intermediary goods (oil, metals, chemicals, and timber) are likely to flood Western markets.

An automatic consequence of the transition to a market economy and free trade will be that the composition of foreign trade will be restructured toward the country's comparative advantages and demands. For Russian exports, this will undoubtedly mean that raw materials and intermediary goods will dominate for years to come. Two other factors will also gradually come into play: cheap labor and an ample supply of technically skilled labor. How fast these factors will gain importance is not yet clear; the more radical, and thus more successful, the systemic change, the sooner they will become significant.

The changes in East European imports provide an indication of what is likely to happen. First, consumer imports will become palpable and cater to starkly neglected consumption through, for instance, imports of used cars. Because trade tends to develop before other sectors of the economy, a multitude of odd new products, such as oriental fruits, will be imported. Early imports will also include medicines and food. As the economy stabilizes and a new private sector develops, more emphasis will go to inputs for production and investment goods. At the outset of the systemic changes, however, rational investment criteria will be absent. Therefore few early investments can be rational, and little investment will be undertaken when left to the market.

Economic Relations between the Russian Government and Former Soviet Republics

The most difficult task politically is also the most important for trade: Russia must clarify its borders and establish what is domestic and what is foreign. Although the USSR belongs to history, many former Soviet citizens find this difficult to comprehend and continue as if it were still in existence. A number of issues, however, need to be resolved as soon as possible.

Top priority should go to clarifying the extent of the ruble zone and establishing a firm monetary authority within that zone. Essentially, the Russian government has pursued appropriate policies on this issue but not decisively enough. In summer 1992, Russia gave the other former Soviet republics a virtual ultimatum: accept the monetary authority of the Central Bank of Russia or withdraw from using the ruble as their domestic currency. The three Baltic states and Ukraine withdrew from the ruble zone and introduced their own currencies in 1992, and Kyrgyzstan followed in May 1993. Belarus was expelled from the ruble zone in November 1992 for having drawn excessive credits from Russia. Georgia, Azerbaijan, Turkmenistan, and Moldova eventually decided to introduce their own currencies in July 1993 in the aftermath of the Russian exchange of banknotes, followed several months later by Armenia, Kazakhstan, and Uzbekistan. Tajikistan remains the only state still willing to accept monetary dictates from Moscow. Once the currency situation is firmly set, orderly payments can be expected and resistance to trade overcome. Nevertheless, the shift by most states from the ruble is less important than a clearly defined monetary authority within each currency area.[4]

Similarly, there is no reason for continuing subsidized trade between the former Soviet republics. A Western country would not voluntarily subsidize exports of competitive products to another Western country. (Agricultural produce and the like form an exception and indicate inclinations of governments to favor certain domestic vested interests at the expense of the welfare of society as a whole.) If trade is to continue without protest from any enterprise involved, free prices must prevail. Any attempt at price controls is likely to cause enterprises to hold back supplies and thus cause shortages, a situation the former USSR has been faced with since 1992.

In the wake of the dissolution of the Soviet Union, a considerable disruption of trade is inevitable because terms of trade are changing and much of the previous trade will turn out to be unprofitable. Indeed, much of the interstate trade has probably been irrational all along. For example, the average haulage of timber on Soviet railways was 1,650 kilometers, which could not be defended in terms of freight costs anywhere in the capitalist world. There is no reason to push this disruption of interstate trade further than necessary, and the creation of markets is the prime objective of systemic change. It is therefore desirable that trade should be as free as possible; that is, trade should not be hindered by the introduction of any licenses, quotas, or tariffs. Given that all the former Soviet republics (apart from the Baltic states) are tardy in their initiation of a market economy, few conflicts should arise around something as simple and easily acceptable as free trade, while any alternative trade regime would cause arguments. Fortunately, there seems to be broad agreement that Russia should endeavor to conclude free trade agreements with all former Soviet republics, and the elaboration of these bilateral agreements has already proceeded far.

An agreement on free trade, however, is not enough to guarantee that trade is actually promoted. A functioning system of payments is also required. A number of similar proposals for the formation of a payments union for the former Soviet Union have been put forward.[5] However, a payments union makes no sense for the former USSR. Nor is one likely to be formed, the main reason being the extraordinary suspicion that persists between the former Soviet republics. In 1992, ruble trade prevailed among most of the new states. But as it became too unbalanced, Russia called for an alteration, because unbalanced trade within the ruble zone amounts to free credits to states that neglect to pay. In the next phase, barter has developed, as first occurred between the Baltic states and Russia, but barter is an extremely inefficient form of exchange. The proliferation of barter is therefore running parallel to a steep decline in trade. As hard currency reserves are gathered, we should expect trade in hard currency to ensue. This is what is happening in Eastern Europe, where internal convertibility or convertibility on current accounts has been introduced. One important advantage of convertibility is that world market prices would prevail in this case. Eventually the former Soviet republics will need to be able to pay one another in their own convertible currencies, and that time may be very close.

As we have already seen in Eastern Europe, the introduction of free prices results in a drastic change in the terms of trade. Russia has benefited greatly from such a change but only in a formal sense: the other republics are not able to continue to buy the same volumes of energy and other raw materials from Russia, and Russia is not able to find alternative markets in the short term. (Admittedly, the current problem is, rather, that the prior export volumes are not even produced.) Considering its precarious financial position, it would be unreasonable to demand that Russia issue substantial credits to the other republics, although limited technical credits might be justified. Instead, all the former Soviet republics have a common interest in the outside world's financing a continuation of trade within the former Soviet Union.

A more general issue is whether multilateral or bilateral agreements between the former Soviet republics are to be preferred. The experiences to date indicate that multilateral agreements are hardly plausible. Indeed, relations between the former Soviet republics only began to get sorted out after June 1992, when Russia concluded that multilateral agreements were no longer possible. This conclusion also renders any kind of payments union less plausible.

There are no reasons for accepting multiple monetary authorities within one currency area, for trade barriers, for fixed prices, or for any significant subsidies to other republics, although there is an obvious need for a payments system and the financing of interstate trade. The ultimate solution must be the introduction of separate, convertible, national currencies. A variety of arguments can be made for and against a common currency, but the heart of the matter is that it must be possible to pursue monetary policy, and that cannot be done under the present political conditions if the ruble area is not split up.

The Russian Government and Its Trade Relations with the Outside World

As discussed earlier, the decision to move to a market economy leads to a number of conclusions. With regard to the whole world outside the former Soviet Union, the natural policy will be free trade. For Russia, it is vital to create proper market relations as soon as possible; protectionism cannot be defended at this stage.[6] In practice, this means that Russia should try to reach free trade agreements with the various trading communities in order of their significance—the European Community (EC), the European Free Trade Area (EFTA), the United States, and Japan—as well as various countries in Eastern Europe and East Asia. No other order of priority appears justified, and the trade agreements may be negotiated in parallel, allowing Russia limited leeway in setting its own priorities. Because of its limited weight in world trade, Russia has an interest in the promotion of multilateral free trade endeavors such as the General Agreement on Tariffs and Trade (GATT) and the Uruguay Round. In particular, the focus should be on freer agricultural trade, because Russia ought to become a major grain exporter in the not too distant future, given its resource endowment. Although trade agreements are concluded with limited trading communities or countries, there is little room for a substantial differentiation in the treatment of different countries. This is particularly true because it is in Russia's interest to establish free trade as soon as possible. Indeed, as Aleksandr Shokhin is in the habit of pointing out, "trade is better than aid."[7]

One special trade restriction directed against Russia, or rather the former USSR, is the Western technology embargo managed by the Coordinating Committee for Multilateral Export Controls (CoCom). Today, it appears impossible to find any rationale for this remnant of the cold war, and it would be natural to abolish all remaining CoCom restrictions as quickly as possible.

Another important issue is financing. The relative success of various countries' attempts to change economic systems is closely related to their degree of access to international financing. The key to international financing is agreements with the International Monetary Fund (IMF). These agreements unleash not only IMF and World Bank financing but all kinds of international financing from the Group of 24 (G–24) and the European Bank for Reconstruction and Development (EBRD). In this connection, Russia received a needed rescheduling of $15 billion of its foreign debt at the April 1993 G–7 finance ministers' meeting in Tokyo and was granted a broader package of possibly $28 billion. In financing, the outside world is acting as a single entity. It is impossible for a debtor in trouble to play one creditor against another. Admittedly, a debtor who is in a reasonably safe situation can bargain over the conditions of loans, but this is within the range of ordinary practice and should not be considered a major policy issue.

Direct foreign investment does not come as easily as many seem to think. Foreign investors will wait until the legal, political, and economic situation is reasonably clarified and stabilized. They want to be reassured of property rights, comprehensive legislation on foreign investment, and legal safeguards for foreign investment, which are generally based on bilateral government agreements. It takes time before such stability can be attained. The size and growth of direct foreign investment is a litmus test for the quality of the systemic change. Although agreements on legal safeguards for foreign investment tend to be bilateral, there is no reason not to conclude such agreements with all interested countries.

An additional issue might be a special payments mechanism for one or several of the neighboring countries. This has previously been discussed in connection with Eastern and central Europe.[8] However, the limited amount of trade is a strong argument against any such multilateral payments union (although an ordinary clearing mechanism with another country—China, for instance—that lacks a sufficient, convertible currency may make sense in a transition period). Mostly, however, the necessary mutual trust is missing.

When the various actual issues at hand are dissected, it becomes clear that Russia does not have available to it all that many choices as to what countries it should turn to. A number of not very glamorous or imaginative trade and finance negotiations have to take place, but their outcome appears fairly obvious. It is in Russia's interest to develop trade and financial relations with as many countries as possible.

Prospects

If the change of economic system is carried out properly, and the course of action suggested above is followed, a number of consequences are likely to ensue. As with the growth of East European exports after a change of economic system, Russian exports should start skyrocketing by 25 to 35 percent in the first year of systemic change, implying export liberalization and domestic stabilization.[9] A second plausible consequence is that trade will expand in the directions of Western Europe and East Asia—neighbors with large domestic markets. Third, trade with most of the developing countries and with former Soviet republics is likely to plummet and stay low for some time. Fourth, the structure of Russia's total exports will change toward larger exports of raw materials.

It would be wrong, however, to imply that Russia's relations with the outside world would follow a predictable course if it only undertook a proper change of economic system. One issue of immense importance—financing— is far from predictable because it is subject to political decisions in the outside world. Financial flows are by no means given, and they can be very small or palpable. At least in the initial stage of a fundamental economic change, these financial flows are more dependent on political than economic decisions.

It is in this field that some vision is needed in the West. The question is, what kind of vision? First, the West needs to consider what kind of body will be the main coordinator of the policies of the outside world toward Russia. At present, the main role is possibly being played by the IMF, which on the one hand is pursuing its role with considerable energy, although there are those who argue that it could be played much better.[10] On the other hand, the role of the IMF is strictly limited to standard economics. It is not supposed to allow itself political leeway or to undertake broader political considerations, even though this is what the outside world really needs in relation to Russia in its current precarious situation. The G–7 is an ad hoc group without any organization or secretariat. Its sherpas are unable to deal with more than one set of problems at a time.

Indeed, the problem is that there is no Western agency that is prepared to play the role of self-evident and attentive world leader with regard to Russia. The Marshall Plan, which provided generous loans on the basis of economic conditionality, played the role of such a body but at the same time functioned as a political umbrella organization. As Eastern Europe and the former Soviet Union proceed with their change of economic system, it is clear both that the transition is quite successful in some countries and that it is really very risky, requiring substantial amounts of outside financial support that only the public sector can provide.

One big difference between today and the period after World War II is that the world no longer has a leading power or even a superpower. This concept lost its meaning at the end of the cold war, when nuclear arms lost most of their implications for international security. The United States no longer appears able or prepared to lead the world, as it was as recently as during the Persian Gulf War in 1991. The Europeans are quarreling as always, unable even to turn sufficient attention to the problem of the former Yugoslavia, while Japan is not yet prepared to take on a major world role. In many regards, the current state of the world is reminiscent of 1922. Then, as now, the old great powers had given up their prior roles before any alternative leading powers had established themselves. The outcome was not a Marshall Plan but plenty of petty bickering. Many parallels can be drawn between Germany in 1922 and Russia today. Germany then was a former power that had lost a large empire without really feeling defeated on the battlefield; the same can be said about today's Russia. Germany fell into severe hyperinflation; Russia is threatened by the same possibility.

What is needed at present is a broad vision of cooperation between the leading market economies of the world and the new market economies in Eastern Europe and the former USSR. Although this essay has focused on Russia in particular, there is no reason why such cooperation should not extend to all of the former Soviet states and all of Eastern Europe as well as the G–24. The main purpose of such a coordinating organization would be to channel financial resources to the eastern part of Europe. But such an organization should also provide technical assistance, set economic conditions, and dare to make political decisions to foster the rebirth of capitalist economies throughout the region. No existing organization appears able to fill this role.

It is difficult to find any reason for Russia to do anything other than carry out the obvious liberalizing measures, without making any particular choice between financial support from the United States, Europe, or East Asia. Therefore it falls on the large wealthy states of the West to put themselves together in a reasonable forum so that they can contribute to the economic and democratic development of Eastern Europe and the former USSR and thus further world stability as well as long-term economic growth. To date, however, the situation in the post–cold war period appears more reminiscent of 1922 than of 1948.

Notes

1. See Janos Kornai, *The Socialist System: The Political Economy of Communism* (Princeton, N.J.: Princeton University Press, 1992), and Anders Åslund, *Gorbachev's Struggle for Economic Reform,* 2nd ed. (London: Pinter, 1991).

2. *Nezavisimaia gazeta,* September 29, 1992, p. 2.

3. *PlanEcon Report,* July 21, 1992, p. 10.

4. Jeffrey Sachs and David Lipton, "Remaining Steps to a Market-Based Monetary System" (Paper presented at the Conference on the Change of Economic System in Russia, Stockholm Institute of East European Economics, June 15–16, 1992).

5. See Oleh Hawrylyshyn and John Williamson, *From Soviet disUnion to Eastern Economic Community?* (Washington, D.C.: Institute for International Economics, 1991), and Daniel Gros, Jean Pisani-Ferry, and André Sapir, eds., *Inter-State Economic Relations in the Former Soviet Union* (Brussels: Centre for European Policy Studies, 1992).

6. David Lipton and Jeffrey Sachs, "Creating a Market in Eastern Europe: The Case of Poland," *Brookings Papers on Economic Activity,* no. 1 (1990): 75–147. For a contrary view, see Ronald I. McKinnon, *The Order of Economic Liberalization* (Baltimore, Md.: Johns Hopkins University Press, 1991).

7. *Izvestiia,* September 16, 1992, p. 5.

8. Peter Bofinger, "A Multilateral Payments Union for Eastern Europe," *CEPR Discussion Paper* (London), no. 458 (1990), and Josef M. van Brabant, "Convertibility in Eastern Europe through a Payments Union," in John Williamson, ed., *Currency Convertibility in Eastern Europe* (Washington, D.C.: Institute for International Economics, 1991), 63–95.

9. Stuart Brown, "Federalism and Marketization in the Soviet Union," in Anders Åslund, ed., *The Post-Soviet Economy: Soviet and Western Perspectives* (London: Pinter, 1992), 132–164.

10. Jeffrey Sachs and David Lipton, "Russia on the Ropes: How the IMF Is Missing Its Chance to Spur Recovery," *Washington Post,* September 29, 1992.

9
Preserving Economic Sovereignty

Aleksandr Shokhin

The solutions to Russia's current problems lie within Russia itself. Yet, in making the transition to a market economy, Russia can learn from the experiences of other countries and can benefit greatly from deeper involvement in the international economy. As Franklin Delano Roosevelt once said, international trade serves any country's "enlightened self-interest." Joining the world economy does not undermine national interests; it strengthens them.

Today, while undergoing its reform process, Russia must balance its increasing integration in the world economy with its economic sovereignty. The rapid acceleration of this integration—in which some fundamental aspects of economic sovereignty become integral components of the international economy—is evident throughout the world. Autarkic notions such as the theory of "two world economies" have become relics of the past.

To avoid facing its economic difficulties alone, Russia is in the process of internationalizing its domestic economic problems. This is an approach that countries with similar problems have used before. Conceivably, this could enable Russia to pursue a prominent role in international economic activities despite its present vulnerability. Russia's current interest lies in increasing the effectiveness of its economic interaction with foreign countries. It must move toward the formation of a market economy, the creation of equal conditions for the development of all forms of property, and the establishment of a stable monetary system.

International Financial Organizations

While ending its isolation from the world economy, Russia's foremost priority remains the preservation of its own national interests. The primary responsibility of the Russian government has been to guide Russia's economic ship between Scylla and Charybdis —that is, between autarky and those people who have attacked this process as the "selling of our Motherland." The practical application of

97

this policy can be seen in Russia's dealings with the International Monetary Fund (IMF) and the International Bank for Reconstruction and Development (IBRD).

The IMF has granted Russia the first half of a new $3 billion "systemic transformation facility" as part of the Western aid package designed by the Group of Seven (G–7) leaders in Tokyo in April 1993. The conditionality of the credit is much lower than that of a standby credit. Half of the credit is targeted for export of strategic resources (such as oil and gas) from Russia to countries of the Commonwealth of Independent States (CIS).

It must be stressed that IMF involvement is essential to the development of a Russian program for financial-economic stabilization. As the Supreme Soviet of the Russian Federation has stated, "the Russian Federation assumes all obligations . . . and will undertake all necessary steps to carry out [IMF agreements]." In doing so, however, Russia will not assume economic policy obligations that contradict its own national interest. All of the IMF's recommendations and policies are to be coordinated with the government. Russia operates on the principle that credit conditionality must coincide with the main directions of government policy concerning the economic and social conditions of the country.

Under international law an agreement between a debtor nation and the IMF is not a binding international agreement. In other words, noncompliance with an IMF agreement is not, strictly speaking, a violation of international law. This does not mean, however, that Russia intends to violate such agreements. Russia recognizes the experience of other countries: the real price of refusing IMF programs is that the cost of failure usually exceeds the socioeconomic and political costs of their implementation. Countries that default on such arrangements have to resume negotiations with the IMF eventually, and they must also adhere to the earlier recommendations of the IMF, which, over time, become more imperative in nature and make more decisive reforms necessary.

Close interaction with both the IMF and the World Bank means that Russia is not simply a passive observer but an active participant in the development of the international monetary system. Russia is thus able to influence strategic decisions in this sphere—an important function for any country integrating into the world economy. From this point of view, it is impossible to accept the belief that participation in the IMF limits a nation's economic sovereignty. Being a member of the international community, Russia can best protect its own national interests by voluntarily undertaking all obligations that follow from the standards and practices of international trade.

Foreign Investment

Attempts to attract foreign capital and to develop a healthy investment climate have previously been characterized unfairly as the economic "enslavement" of a country and the eventual denial of its sovereignty. Such views have been proved naive and shortsighted. In the United States, for example, foreign investment has reached enormous sums, but serious politicians do not usually object that the influx of capital brings political costs; they welcome it. Such issues are regulated by local legislation that supports and protects the national interest. Currently, the legislation of Russia is in the process of developing in this direction.

History has shown that it is not necessary to create any special conditions to attract direct foreign investment. Nondiscriminatory trade policies are sufficient. This includes normalization of trade as a whole, including the removal of discriminatory restrictions on Russian exporters. In addition, it is important to provide a stable economic and political situation in Russia as well as the proper financial infrastructure for international trade. At the present time, Russian laws on foreign investment are in accordance with these principles and the new order of foreign economic activities. A climate for foreign investors must be created in which there is no fear of wasting material, financial, and intellectual resources in the Russian economy.

The Russian Agency for International Cooperation and Development was created specifically for attracting foreign investment. Offices within the agency include the Fund for Political Risk Insurance, the Center for Project Financing Investment, and the Agency for Technical Assistance. This does not mean, however, that all investors must pass through the "bottleneck" of the agency. On the contrary, investors can choose for themselves with whom they wish to deal.

In the end, the flow of foreign capital (about $800 million per year) is an insignificant part of the total volume of investment in Russia. There is no clear and present danger of "selling off" the Russian economy to foreign capital. According to the most favorable estimates, the percentage of foreign investment in Russia in the total volume of investments will be only 2 to 3 percent. In contrast, Hungary is seeking to raise the share of foreign investment in its economy to 25 percent. For Russia, such a goal is unrealistic: there is simply not enough capital in the world to reach a level of 25 percent of the investment in Russia. To achieve that would require more than $20 billion a year in foreign investment alone, yet in 1991 the net flow of foreign capital into all developing countries from Western Europe accounted for only $31 billion.

Investment Projects

Although investments in Russia are full of potential, serious political risks and the current economic crisis undermine these possibilities. Russia currently has a number of multibillion dollar projects in such sectors of the economy as the oil and gas, construction, food, and fishing industries. Among the projects of national importance vis-à-vis foreign investment, the largest and most comprehensive is the privatization of state property. Russia has much to offer to foreign investors, but the need to prevent the hasty and inequitable sale of state property is clear.

Obviously, Russia's main interest is in working with firms that have serious intentions and are ready to invest their capital for a long period. The Russian government also wants to bring different investors to different fields of the economy and regions of Russia. This policy seeks to prevent foreign companies from developing into new monopolies.

One very important point should be mentioned here: Russia's interest in foreign investment is not unconditional. The Russian government controls and will continue to control investments in the oil and gas, coal-mining, and defense industries. Government regulation of foreign investment in Russia is aimed not only at stimulating investments from abroad but also at protecting Russia's economic security and sovereignty.

The protection of national security is crucial to the realization of economic sovereignty. There are three main areas of economic regulation: hard currency control, export-import control, and licensing of strategic raw materials.

Introduction of a strict hard currency regime is one of the necessary means for averting the danger of massive capital outflow from the country. One of Russia's most pressing problems is capital flight. Current estimates of this problem go as high as $15 to $20 billion per year and higher. How can Russia correct this situation? Escaping capital will return only when there are attractive conditions for investors within the domestic economy. In addition, improved legislative regulation of currency operations, accounting procedures, and tax structure is needed. The Russian government must create conditions under which Russian entrepreneurs want to invest in Russia.

A law on currency regulation must become the basis for the activities of the Central Bank of the Russian Federation, the recently created Federal Currency and Export Control Service, and the State Customs Committee. An expert control and licensing system for exports of military and dual-use technologies will be simultaneously introduced. A new system of state control over exports of arms and armaments will also be brought into action.

The next step in consolidating currency control will be the introduction of regulations on the export of strategic raw materials. Before the government decree restricting the export of such materials, some strategic raw materials were sold on the world market at prices 5 to 10 times lower than the world average. The new measures will be executed by qualified structures that possess adequate personnel to enforce established export taxes and guarantee the repatriation of profits. These measures are aimed mainly at controlling the foreign trade of strategic fuels and raw materials without restoring state monopolies over the process. Any economic unit may be granted the right for foreign trade. At the same time, the trade of strategic raw materials will be conducted only via specially registered foreign trade companies. Thus not only will effective currency control be possible, but price control mechanisms can be created to prevent dumping. A similar order will allow Russia to facilitate exporters' settlements with the state budget.

Foreign Debt

Russia's foreign debt (officially about $80 billion) is a potential threat to the country's economic sovereignty. It is obvious that the Russian government must seek ways to settle the problem. There are, however, certain hidden complications such as exchange of debt for equity, participation of foreign creditors in privatization, and provision of concessions to cover indebtedness, as proposed by Boris Yeltsin at the G–7 meeting in Munich in July 1992. The greatest fears caused by the existing ruble-to-dollar exchange rate concern the possibility that foreign proprietors may gain control over the greatest part of Russia's national resources and, thus, control over key fields of its economy.

Such fears about the debt problem are not groundless. The experience of Eastern Europe, in fact, justifies them. At the same time, alternatives for settling the problem provide a real basis for future development, with the influx of investments and the possibility of reducing the debt without spiraling inflation. The possibility of finding a way out of the debt crisis and resuming normal economic development by converting the debt into equity is justified by the experience of Mexico and Chile. But Russia is at the beginning of that path. It has only recently—in spring 1993—been granted a $15 billion debt rescheduling, marking the first serious step to support Russian reforms. Rescheduling of the foreign debt of the former USSR will create a solid financial base for continuation of economic reforms in Russia. Still, more needs to be done.

Weeding out hostile foreign currency traders is essential. Fears about the debt problem could also be allayed through increased budget revenues and greater investments in plants and factories, including better working conditions for Russian personnel. It is also desirable that foreign companies with adequate expertise participate in the process of privatization; when selling an enterprise to foreign investors, the state should be certain that the purchaser can provide for its efficient functioning.

The question of joint responsibility for covering the foreign debt of the USSR remains a serious problem. Of the former republics, however, only Russia is capable of dealing with payments of old debts. It would be best for creditors to negotiate the debts of the USSR with the Russian Federation only, while the Russian government determines the amount of mutual debts. This idea has been accepted by virtually all of the states of the former Soviet Union, although some details remain to be worked out with Ukraine. Agreements with Belarus, Turkmenistan, and Kyrgyzstan, for example, under which Russia assumes their percentages of the foreign debt while they renounce their shares in foreign assets, have already been signed.

Economic Relations with the CIS

An important aspect of Russian economic security is the regulation of trade and economic relations with the former republics of the USSR. In fact, the regulation of payment-settlement and monetary-credit relations with the newly independent states remains Russia's most pressing economic problem. The key prerequisite to resolving this issue is the acknowledgment of the foreign economic nature of these relations. Trade and financial relations with these states should, while taking into account the historical background, be based on the principles applied to any other foreign country. After all, trading with these countries at internal prices would amount to subsidizing the former Soviet states to the tune of billions of dollars.

The recent past has shown that a policy aimed at the preservation of the common ruble zone has no future. The interests of Russia's sovereignty demanded that the CIS members introduce their own national currencies, as all but Tajikistan have done. This decision has clarified considerably the obligations these countries should assume, as exemplified by an agreement between Russia and Lithuania. The step-by-step program of monetary stabilization proposed earlier by Russia is widely considered to be the most logical and realistic course.

Discussing transition to a payment union is the next step. Such a mechanism was used quite effectively in postwar Europe and may work in Russia today. A transition means, first of all, the realization of multilateral trade transactions without any obstacles, stabilization of the monetary systems to allow currency convertibility, and overall intensification of economic development. The Eurasian Settlement Chamber can play an active role in the payment union, executing the main part of the multilateral settlements among the participants.

One of the primary guarantees of economic sovereignty is the establishment of customs boundaries. On March 13, 1992, Armenia, Belarus, Kazakhstan, Moldova, Russia, Tajikistan, Turkmenistan, and Uzbekistan signed a treaty addressing the principles of the customs policy and a statute on the customs councils. The treaty presupposes the introduction of a duty-free exchange regime for goods and services as well as the establishment of a customs union. Subsequently, Ukraine, Russia, and Belarus signed a draft treaty on July 1, 1993, in Minsk on closer economic integration.

Yet some of the states seem unprepared for a common customs union. For example, a number of them rejected the agreements, while others took up measures that contradicted the logic of the union. As a result, Russia has been forced to take measures to halt the reexport of Russian products, such as oil, gas, and nonferrous and rare metals, by the former Union republics. Although its losses resulting from Ukrainian reexports of oil and chemical fertilizers are quite high, Russia's reaction remains mild for the moment. When the drafts of the 1993 treaties on trade and economic cooperation between Russia and the other former Union republics were being prepared, it was proposed that Ukraine should participate in the development of the energy resources of Russia. Such an arrangement might lead to a new increase in the low energy supplies to Ukraine.

Large amounts of oil products, metals, fertilizers, and grain are going from Russia to the Baltic states without licenses and customs documentation. Under an agreement between the Baltics and Russia, work has begun on equipping the stationary control posts on their shared borders. The customs control regime to be used there will be the same as is used with any other foreign state. Russia has stringent agreements with all the CIS countries to control reexport, allowing it only if permission is granted in writing by the Russian side.

On October 1, 1992, 64 customs posts began functioning on Russia's borders with the Baltic states, Ukraine, Azerbaijan, and Georgia. These steps will make it possible to bring order to economic relations in the CIS and start the next stage in the liberalization of foreign economic activities.

Conclusion

The most constructive way to strengthen the economic sovereignty of Russia and stabilize the situation there is to bring to life the formula "Trade, rather than aid." This notion was put forth some time ago by the deputy chairman of the Committee of European Communities, F. Andriessen. Others have adopted it, and the Russian government supports it strongly.

Today, discriminatory quotas on Russian exports are costing Russia potential profits for which it receives only partial compensation through foreign aid and credits. The elimination of these and other restrictions, including the Coordinating Committee for Multilateral Export Controls (CoCom), will further facilitate Russia's integration into the world economy. The whole complex of these measures will allow the Russian Federation to play an important role in the world economy.

The Russian government is united in its commitment to further economic reform. The people of Russia support and understand the importance of this policy. Of course, in a democracy opposing views are to be expected, and the Russian government is willing to discuss changes in its position. But it must be repeated—the integration of Russia's domestic economy into the world economy is a fundamental aspect of Russia's national interest. As it assumes the obligations of integration into the world economy and creates favorable conditions for foreign investors, however, Russia intends at the same time to protect its sovereign economic interests.

10
Russia and Its Interests

Vladimir P. Lukin

The starting point for any discussion about the interests of Russia has to be a discussion about Russia itself. What kind of country are we talking about—territorially, politically, and ideologically? The current process of self-determination in Russia is far from complete. Recent history suggests at least three possible paths for the future: Russia could become a democratic nation-state, or an authoritarian empire, or it could collapse into small, weak, fragments at war with one another.

The last path is possible, unfortunately, but there is little point in examining the interests of such a Russia. A replay of the internal wars of Russian history in the fourteenth and fifteenth centuries— on a grander scale, of course, and with qualitatively new levels of weaponry—would be a tragedy for the citizens of Russia and for the entire world.

The second path is also possible (in part because of the growing threat of the first), but historically it leads to a dead end. Rigid authoritarianism in Russia would be an evil anachronism that would waste the country's capacity for social and economic dynamism.

The first course—consolidation into a democratic nation-state— would not only be the best result, but also the only one that would allow Russia to remain a great power and become a member of the community of developed nations.

Which path Russia chooses will depend primarily on the people of Russia themselves. Primarily, but not entirely. Neighbors both near and far will play a significant role and that role (which I will discuss below) could have many different results. But, first, we should take up these questions: What would a strong and democratic Russia look like, and what would be its national interests?

Democracy in Russia is in some ways similar to the American, or Western, model, but there are many differences as well. The development of a national political system is a deeply internal, intimate, and somewhat arbitrary process for any nation. The process is rooted in history, in national character, and in the nation's political talent. In Russia the process is not nearly as hopeless as is sometimes stated. Despite its very difficult history, Russia does possess a democratic and liberal tradition. Although long suppressed, this tradition has survived to play a part in Russia's current attempt to create its own democratic institutions. Russia will proceed toward democracy, if it proceeds at all, on its own path—-slowly and tortuously removing authoritarianism and super-centralization from its political organism.

To judge by Russia's traditions and the objective qualities of the country, the institutions of the Russian state must be strong if they are to be effective. Such strong institutions would not necessarily suppress democracy as long as they are periodically passed through the gauntlet of free elections, limited in their powers, justified in their actions by law, based on an internal balance of power, and moderated by an independent press. In one form or another, each of these conditions is being met in Russia today. The strengthening of democracy and its conversion into an effective system of administration for the entire country represent Russia's most important national interest.

The next question concerns Russian national statehood *(gosudarstvennost')*, a term that by itself can lead to some confusion. Russia has always been a multinational state in which the Great Russian majority mixed, both geographically and ethnically, with dozens of other peoples. Interethnic borders were drawn artificially and arbitrarily. Like it or not, this centuries-old hodgepodge is the difficult reality of Russian life. To attempt to define "ethnically pure" borders in these conditions, even in the name of national self-determination, is to make refugees of tens of millions of people, destroy millions of families, and still not achieve ethnic purity: in almost every Russian there is some Ukrainian, some Tatar, and vice versa.

Complete national-ethnic self-determination would lead directly to the dissolution of Russia into smaller and smaller pieces isolated from one another. The only way to avoid that is through a decisive policy—not just gestures but an actual policy—that preserves and strengthens a single federal state, guarantees equal rights for all citizens, and respects national and ethnic diversity. The strengthening of unity and territorial integrity is, in my opinion, another fundamental "national interest" of Russia; it is a necessary condition for national democratic development.

A "Good Neighbor" Policy

The next obvious interest of Russia—one that all other states pursue—is its interest in security and, in particular, good relations with its neighbors. The West—and especially the United States, with its rich experience of relations with weak neighbors in the Western Hemisphere—can understand that what Russians call the "near abroad" is a zone of fundamentally important interests and a natural sphere of Russia's influence. The real question is, how will this influence be exercised? The answer, visible from our history, depends above all on the political structure of Russia itself.

Czarism, for all its rigidity, protected the national and cultural autonomy of its hinterlands and made use of traditional institutions. Stalinism, because of its totalitarian nature, saw security only in terms of complete control over Russia's neighbors. This was accomplished by transforming them into satellites on the Soviet model. Democratic Russia is not afraid of the sovereignty and independence of its new neighbors; in fact, Russia helped them become independent. It is not now going to force them to adopt its own form of government, nor will it interfere in their internal affairs. At the same time, Russia is entitled to expect them to respect and uphold the human and civil rights of the Russian-speaking residents of their territory. This condition is, in fact, much more important for democratic Russia than it was under Stalinism. Russia is also justified in expecting its neighbors to prevent threats to Russia from arising on their territory as a result of the activities of third countries. Russia is prepared to provide them with any cooperation necessary to establish their own security, through both bilateral and multilateral arrangements.

Such interaction between a strong country and its weak neighbors is nothing other than a "good neighbor" policy. This is a policy well known to Americans, who have long practiced it on the basis of such agreements as the Monroe Doctrine and the Rio Pact. Russia's good neighbor policy will, of course, be unique—with variations that reflect the enormous differences among the states on its borders. Some of those countries will have closer ties to Russia than others. All the same, the good neighbor policy must serve as the foundation of Russia's foreign policy orientation. The construction of such relations is a difficult process; it requires much responsibility, thought, patience, and political innovation from all its participants, and primarily from Russia. In my opinion, however, there are no insurmountable obstacles to making this policy work.

It is not only Russia that must adjust to this new reality, but the "far abroad" as well. Other major powers can influence—either positively or negatively—the formation of relations between Russia and its neighbors. The West must maintain its objectivity and not allow memories of the past to cloud its interpretation of the actions of today's Russia. It should not see the "resurrection of the empire" or a "re-centralization of the Union" in every energetic step that Russia takes to protect its interests or in attempts at cooperation in the area of security. Obviously, such reflexive responses to Russian policy have deep historical roots. The best way to avoid them is for Russia to conduct a truly "post-imperial" policy that advances its interests as we understand them today, not simply as we understood them in the past.

In sum, keeping the territory of the Commonwealth of Independent States (CIS) stable through good-neighborliness and collective security serves the security interests of Russia itself and those of its neighbors. Maintaining stability also serves the interests of other powers, including the United States, which is the main external player in the strategic balance of Eurasia.

Russia's Foreign Policy beyond the "Near Abroad"

Beyond the "near abroad," the foreign policy interests of Russia are strongest in those areas of the world in which it functions as a multiregional Eurasian power: central and northern Europe, the Indian subcontinent, the Middle East, and the Pacific Rim region. In all these areas Russia has deep, historic interests that need to be protected not only to avoid regional imbalances, but also to prevent the disruption of the social and political balance inside Russia itself. Russia simply cannot allow itself to adopt an exclusively "Atlantic" or "Asian" orientation in foreign policy.

In Europe, Russia's primary interest lies in improving relations with the European Community and gradual integration into the European economic and political system. At the same time, Russia is opposed to the transformation of Europe into a closed economic system and military-political union, just as it would oppose the appearance of a dominant regional power. For Russia, it is best to preserve both the multipolar nature of European politics and the role of the United States in the region.

Russia's long-term interests in the Far East involve preserving good relations with Japan, the People's Republic of China, and the other countries of the region and preventing any one of those countries from exerting a controlling influence in the area. In particular, Russia must give its political and economic relations with China footing equal to its relations with Europe and the United States. Russia's goal here should be to establish "irreversible interdependence," in which neither country could return to a policy of direct confrontation with the other.

To the south, Russia's primary interest lies in preventing open conflict with third countries for influence in the developing vacuum of Central Asia and the Transcaucasus. Turkey, Iran, and Afghanistan are already involved in the region, and the role of China and other South Asian countries should not be discounted. It is important, in other words, not to focus simply on the spread of Islamic fundamentalism, but to see possible military confrontation between Islamic, Christian, and Asian civilizations. The possible Balkanization of Russia's southern "underbelly" is full of colossal threats not only for Russia's security but for the strategic stability of all of Eurasia.

Democratic Russia, if it meets with cooperation from the West, can play an important, stabilizing role because of its unique, centuries-old experience of relations with these three worlds. Much thought must be given to this issue, but one clear possibility would be for Russia to form a system of collective security for the southern CIS while simultaneously developing mutually beneficial relations with its primary southern neighbors. Once again, it should be recognized by all that the reestablishment of Russia's stabilizing role is in the interest of not only the regional powers but the international community as a whole. Within such a strategic framework,

Russia would favor an increased role for institutions such as the Conference on Security and Cooperation in Europe (CSCE).

Russia's National Interest vis-à-vis the United States

Relations with the United States unquestionably remain one of the most important aspects of Russian foreign policy. Russia is interested in close, long-term cooperation with the United States for a number of reasons, but primarily because America, despite its disputable "fall," remains (in part because of Russia's undisputed—but, I believe, temporary—decline) the leading political-military force in the world. As such, it can facilitate or complicate Russian policy throughout the world. America's possibilities in this respect are much greater than those of any other country, given that no other power has so much freedom of action, either in setting its goals or in selecting the means to achieve them.

To speak of a Russian interest in cooperating with the United States does not mean anything as broad as a Russian-U.S. condominium, nor as narrow as economic assistance (which Russia also needs). What is essential is U.S. support for Russia's progress toward democracy and market economics on the basis of recognition of legitimate security interests. Without this, reform will be impossible. The young Russian democracy will not succeed if it is surrounded by permanent instability. And if Russian democracy does not succeed—and there should be no illusions here—then the entire wave of contemporary democratization in Eurasia may also fail.

If democracy does begin to fail, what would happen to Russia's strategy toward the outside world? One clear possibility would be an alliance with activists of the developing world, designed to play on the contradictions among the great powers—in particular, Japan, Germany, the United States, and China. Russia would, in effect, switch to pursuing its basic security interests in defiance of, rather than in cooperation with, the United States. Such a policy would make these interests seem more rigid, more "imperial" in form.

Neither of Russia's options will materialize overnight; each would require a great deal of effort before it is put in place. In fact, even now work is going on in both directions, and the long-term choice still remains open. In both Russia and the United States, there are vocal opponents of a Russian-U.S. partnership. In Russia, there are the extreme patriots who feel that a morally corrupt United States is not deserving of friendship with Great Russia. In the United States, the opponents of partnership are the fundamentalist believers in realpolitik, who hold that rivalry between great powers is the essence of world politics and that Russia is an inherently aggressive, expansionist, and now-weak state. In their view, Russia does not deserve partners. Both of these camps ruin the political atmosphere domestically and abroad; they unintentionally boost each other. In Russia, the result is to strengthen xenophobia and anti-American paranoia.

There are, however, some aspects of Russia's relations with the United States that have done as much harm to the cause of cooperation as have its committed opponents. For some Americans and even some Russians, partnership is a relationship between a Russian child and an American father. The United States is seen as the only means of salvation for Russia, which must for this reason extend unconditional support for any U.S. initiative. This outlook has created an unfortunate impression in the Russian national consciousness (which has already suffered greatly): partnership is seen as a one-way street in which Russian interests are sacrificed to those of a foreign country, as a result compromising the very notion of a Russian-U.S. partnership.

To some extent, romantic, infantile pro-Americanism can be explained as a response to the massive confrontation that took place during the cold war. The inertia of that time meant that Russia stopped thinking about itself, and Americans stopped thinking about Russia or worrying about winning its support. Inertia led both sides into an easy, mindless existence in which Russia's foreign policy was taken for granted.

Unfortunately, this trend allowed unrealistic expectations to take root in the United States. A psychological habit developed that makes it difficult to understand the movement of Russian policy toward greater independence. What should be seen as a natural and necessary correction is instead feared as an ill-intentioned departure from the democratic reform policy of rapprochement with the West.

Nevertheless, the transition to a long-term, balanced policy in the Russian-U.S. partnership is necessary. This policy, under the conditions of today's democratic Russia, must be balanced within the country and must have widespread support among political figures and the population as a whole. This, in my opinion, demands a new level of thinking about foreign policy. Such a policy must evolve outside the traditional dichotomy between foreign policy realism and foreign policy idealism. It must find a middle ground between these two poles.

"Realism," if taken to its logical conclusion, ceases to be realistic and becomes instead an "ideology of realism." By ideology, I mean a false concept that explains phenomena by taking only one side of a complex subject and consciously ignoring the others for the sake of theoretical construction and simplicity. *Hyper*-realism ignores ideal (especially sociopsychological) motives and the constantly changing dynamics of international relations in favor of strength and geopolitical factors. By ignoring ideas, realism itself becomes an ideology, a dogma.

"Idealism" goes to the opposite extreme: it ignores balance-of-power motives and impulses. As a consequence, it too becomes "ideologized" and obscures the complex nature of global politics. On the Russian side, the result is neo-Cominternism; in America, it is neo-Wilsonianism.

In the past, neither of these schools could by itself adequately explain global politics or provide a useful compass for national policy. This is even more true on the eve of the twenty-first century. The modern world, more diverse and multifaceted than ever before, is a world of postmodern global interdependence and medieval neanderthal geopolitics; of secular rationality and religious fundamentalism; of integrated economics, information, and even ideology (free markets and democracy) and sharply different standards of living.

As a result, it is necessary to be able to play simultaneously on several "chess boards"—the geo-political, the geo-economic, and the geo-ideological. Each board has its own figures, its own rules, and its own stakes. Too frequently, though, the players do not look beyond their first move. All of this seriously complicates the intellectual development of a new concept of world politics and national interests, including Russian-American relations. It also makes this work more real and more necessary.

Returning to the problem of a Russian-U.S. strategic partnership, I will put forth the traditional question: Is it in the interests of the United States to help democratic Russia realize its national interests and stand on its feet again as a major power? Americans themselves must answer this question, but I believe that the only possible answer is affirmative. The long-term interest of the United States in its relations with Russia is to assist in Russia's transformation into a democratic power—sovereign and fully part of the civilized world. Everything else should be seen in relation to this primary goal. In the transformation of Russia that is under way, Russians are prepared to listen to advice and to consider U.S. interests carefully and constructively, but they themselves must make the main decisions about what to do and how to do it.

Forty years ago, George Kennan was asked how the United States might realistically expect to view Russia after the cold war. In his article "America and the Russian Future" (published in April 1951 in *Foreign Affairs*), Kennan wrote that such a Russia would be rid of totalitarianism and its empire and would open up to the outside world. In the last several years, Russia has not only made amazing strides in this direction but actually surpassed many of Kennan's expectations. This fact provides the main internal guarantee against a return to the traditional "Russo-Soviet threat." It makes even a strong Russia safe and friendly for the West and, in particular, the United States.

If we are to discuss the idealistic side of the issue then we cannot tolerate illusions. The formation of democracy in Russia will be difficult. If it succeeds, then it will also succeed in many of the countries of Eastern Europe and the CIS. If democracy fails in Russia, the result will be a long and dangerous period of authoritarianism, and perhaps fascism, in Russia and elsewhere. This is the historical logic of the "domino theory" in Eurasia. (The same logic, it should be noted, works in Latin America as well: much depends on which movement—authoritarianism or democracy—succeeds in Brazil and Argentina.)

On the realpolitik side of the issue, Russia will retain a key role in the long-term balance of power in Europe. The North Atlantic Treaty Organization (NATO) was a U.S. reaction to a strong, aggressive Russia (at that time, the USSR) and a weak Germany. Continuing a NATO-like policy at a time when Germany is strong and Russia is weak is not politics but inertia. It can lead only to the destabilization of Eastern Europe all the way to the Urals and to the growing "Germanization" of Europe rather than the "Europeanization" of Germany. Such a Western policy of inertia might play itself out in different ways, among them a kind of "super-Rapallo," which would hardly suit long-term U.S. interests.

There is a way out. It lies in creating a new European community (along the lines of François Mitterrand's proposed confederation) that would operate according to rules established by the club of democratic countries. In such a community, new balances would protect Russian interests and U.S. interests as well. Democratic Russia would balance any pro-German influence in Eastern Europe. Constructive U.S. participation would curtail any traditional Russian involvement in the region should it develop, although I think that highly unlikely in the foreseeable future.

As for Asia, a stable, democratic Russia will clearly support U.S. interests in the geopolitical space of the CIS. Russia will be a real partner in the constructive containment of Islamic fundamentalism. In the Far East, the strengthening of Japan and other pretenders to the role of dominant regional power will provide additional reasons for a close Russian-U.S. partnership.

On the geo-economic board, Russia is not only a large long-term market for goods and investment, but also—because of its geographic location—a potential link between the three developing trade and economic super-regions—Europe, Asia, and North America.

The list of positive characteristics of a Russian-U.S. partnership could be even longer. Of course, there will be many problems and obstacles in creating it. For this reason it is necessary for the two countries to define their common national interests and to make them the foundation of current policies.

Let me sum up. Strategically, Russia needs the United States. But the United States also needs Russia. Russians understand this very well and, because we understand it, are ready for a serious discussion about how to create a real partnership between Russia and the United States. If based on equality and respect, such a partnership will yield continuing benefits for both countries.

CSIS BOOKS of Related Interest

Post-Communist Politics: Democratic Prospects in Russia and Eastern Europe
Michael McFaul

In the fourth volume in CSIS's special series *Creating the Post-Communist Order*, Michael McFaul examines the transitions from authoritarian to democratic rule in Poland, Czechoslovakia, Hungary, and—most important—Russia. He analyzes the formation and consolidation of post-Communist political institutions, with special emphasis on the role of social movements, parties, and civil society.

". . . a wealth of details and insights that will surely be noticed by other students of the region. . . . [The] two chapters on building the Russian state and parties are invaluable."
 — Comparative Politics

CSIS *Significant Issues Series*	132 pp.	1993	$14.95

Other titles in the series:
Post-Communist Economic Revolutions: How Big a Bang?
Anders Åslund

	106 pp.	1992	$9.95

The Last Leninists: The Uncertain Future of Asia's Communist States
Robert A. Scalapino

	112 pp.	1992	$14.95

Red Armies in Crisis
Bruce D. Porter

	112 pp.	1991	$14.95

- -

Order Form   Subtotal _____
Postage and handling   _____ 3.50

All orders must be prepaid or charged.   **Total** _____

☐ Check (payable to CSIS)
☐ VISA ☐ MASTERCARD ☐ AMEX   Exp. date _____

Card No. _____
Name on card _____
Signature _____ Phone: _____
Send books to _____
_____
_____
_____

CSISBOOKS 1800 K Street, N.W. Suite 400 Washington, D.C. 20006
Telephone (202) 775-3119 Fax (202) 775-3190